I0308904

Principles of
MICROECONOMICS

CLEP* Study Guide

All rights reserved. This Study Guide, Book and Flashcards are protected under the US Copyright Law. No part of this book or study guide or flashcards may be reproduced, distributed or stored in a retrieval system, or transmitted in any form or by any means, electronic, mechanical, photocopying, recording, or otherwise, without the prior written permission of the publisher Breely Crush Publishing, LLC.

© 2019 Breely Crush Publishing, LLC

*CLEP is a registered trademark of the College Entrance Examination Board which does not endorse this book.

971092018143

Copyright ©2003 - 2019, Breely Crush Publishing, LLC.

All rights reserved.

This Study Guide, Book and Flashcards are protected under the US Copyright Law. No part of this publication may be reproduced, distributed or stored in a retrieval system, or transmitted in any form or by any means, electronic, mechanical, photocopying, recording, or otherwise, without the prior written permission of the publisher Breely Crush Publishing, LLC.

Published by Breely Crush Publishing, LLC
10808 River Front Parkway
South Jordan, UT 84095
www.breelycrushpublishing.com

ISBN-10: 1-61433-581-8
ISBN-13: 978-1-61433-581-8

Printed and bound in the United States of America.

*CLEP is a registered trademark of the College Entrance Examination Board which does not endorse this book.

Table of Contents

Basic Economic Concepts *1*
   Scarcity the Nature of Economic Systems *1*
   Opportunity Costs and Productive Possibilities *1*
   Comparative Advantage *3*

The Nature and Function of the Product Market *4*
   Supply and Demand *4*
      Demand, Supply and Price Determination *4*
   Consumer Demand *7*
   Diminishing Marginal Benefit *8*
   Consumer's Surplus *9*
   Shift in Demand Curve *11*
   Elasticity of Demand *12*
   Firm's Production Cost and Revenue *13*
   Revenue *18*
      Long Run Costs and Economies of Scale *20*
      Long Period Total Cost Curves *20*
      Economies of Scale *21*
   Profit Maximization: Pricing, Revenue and Output Both In the
   Long Run and the Short Run and In the Firm and the Market *22*
      Perfect Competition *22*
      Monopolistic Competition *23*
      Monopoly *24*
      Efficiency *25*

Factor Market *25*
   Derived Demand *25*
   Determination of Wages and Other Factors of Production *26*
   Distribution of Income *27*

Market Failures and the Role of Government *27*
     Externalities, Public Good and Information Economics *27*
      Externalities: a.k.a. Spillover or Third Party Effect *27*
      Public Good *28*

Graphs To Know *30*
Sample Test Questions *32*
Test-Taking Strategies *62*
What Your Score Means *62*
Test Preparation *63*
Legal Note *63*

Basic Economic Concepts

SCARCITY THE NATURE OF ECONOMIC SYSTEMS

As per principles of "Macroeconomics," there are distinct systems: (1) Capitalism (2) Socialism and (3) Mixed economy. We will study each separately later.

OPPORTUNITY COSTS AND PRODUCTIVE POSSIBILITIES

Opportunity Costs is only a notional cost. It is concerned with Comparative rather than actual costs. In economics, it is referred to in respect to a particular choice. It is equal to the value of the next best choice or alternative. An economist sees the costs arising out of doing a 'certain thing' rather than 'another' and compares the opportunities foregone in persisting with that 'certain thing' in relation to that 'another'. Suppose the costs of doing performing choice 'X' is $10 and the next alternative 'Y' is $5, then other things being equal by persisting with choices 'X', we are sacrificing $5, which amounts to a foregone opportunity of $5. If we switched over to alternative 'Y' opportunity cost is not real; it is only notional. It stems from analysis of alternatives.

Let us take the case of a very small country "A." It has a choice either to produce automobiles or wheat for consumption. What are the Production Possibilities?

CHOICES	AUTOMOBILES (IN MILLIONS)	WHEAT (IN MILLION TONS)
A	0	15
B	1	14
C	2	12
D	3	9
E	4	5
F	5	0

Principles of Microeconomics

It can be graphically represented thus:

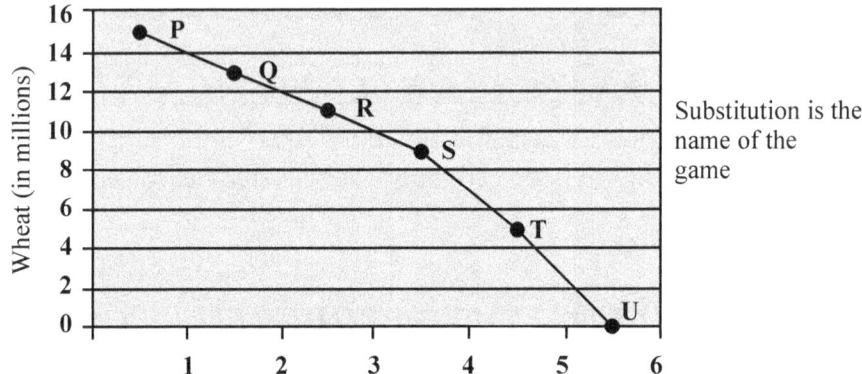

Substitution is the name of the game

This is the country "A's" production possibilities of automobiles and wheat. If they choose zero automobiles during a given period of time, then they can produce 15 million tons of wheat. On the other side of the spectrum, country "A" can choose to produce zero wheat in which case they can produce 5 million automobiles. The various choices they can have are indicated in the above production choice frontier. Let us now consider two situations:

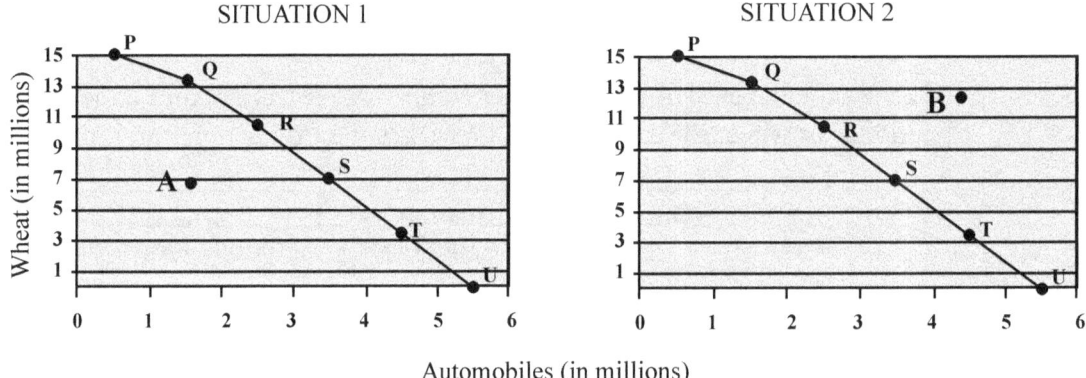

Other things being equal, in a given availability of resources and in a given state of technology, country "A's" menu of choices of automobiles vis-à-vis wheat is represented in the curve P, Q, R, S, T, U. Any point inside this curve like point "A" in the graph indicates that the resources are not being utilized optimally. In the case of unemployment of resources - land, labor, machinery and material - we are bound to be inside the production choice graph - not on it. This is depicted in the graph of "Situation 1."

An economy **cannot** operate at any point outside its production choice graph. The graph depicting point "B" in "Situation 2," therefore, cannot happen. Let us now consider another situation:

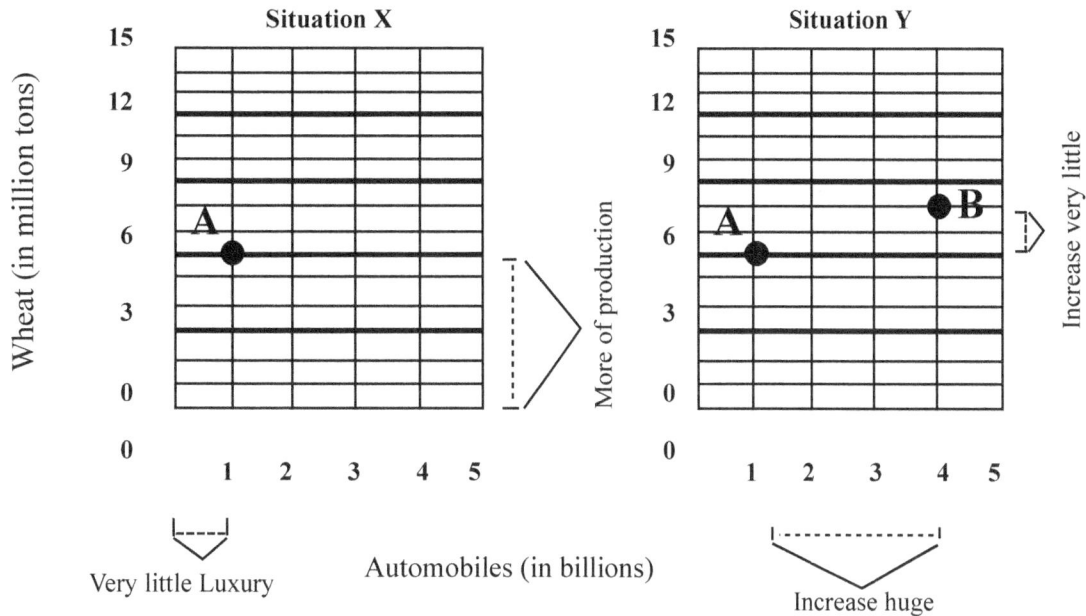

When the country was poor, it could not think of automobiles (even lower-income countries have a few high-income groups which spend lavishly), and therefore concentrated on production of food mainly. When the same country started developing, the food production improved very little but the production of automobiles jumped. We have shown "Automobiles" only for the sake of continuation of our previous illustrations. You may take it as units of "comforts" or "luxuries."

COMPARATIVE ADVANTAGE

A product is always produced in the place that is best suited for its manufacture. In other words there is an age-old tendency to produce a given good in a given area, which is bestowed with an absolute advantage in the production of that good compared to all other areas. There are regions in every country that specialize in producing a par- ticular good. Within the same country it would be uneconomical for other regions to produce that product/good. Over the years skills have been developed and producing a particular good has become a specialty of that region. So, specialization brings gains. What is good for an individual, a town, or, a region within a country holds good for trade between countries as well.

Many countries are producing similar products in their countries for home consumption. Just as individuals trade only if there is an advantage - a profit - so do countries. Nations trade because they expect to profit from their trading associates.

Adam Smith, in his wonderful book "Wealth of Nations" propounded the theory of "absolute advantage." Briefly stated, this theory tells us that a given country should export a product, which can be produced at a cost lower than at what cost the other trading nations can make it; by the same token, it also reveals that the same country should import a product, which can only be made at a cost much higher than the other trading nations can make it.

David Ricardo in his excellent Book "The Principles of Political Economy and Taxation" argues that the absolute production costs are irrelevant, but what is relevant and meaningful is the relative production costs that determine which products are to be imported and which are to be exported. This is known as "the principle of relative (a.k.a. comparative) advantage." Though a country like India is good at producing many products, its exports should be concentrated more on information technology-related products where it has exceptional competence compared to others. Here, the comparative advantages are determined by relative richness as well as abundance of factor endowments. (The "theory of factor endowments" by Eli Heckscher, is in "interregional and international trade.")

The Nature and Function of the Product Market

SUPPLY AND DEMAND

DEMAND, SUPPLY AND PRICE DETERMINATION

What is "Total Utility"? The total utility is the gross psychological satisfaction a consumer derives from consuming a given quantity of a particular good. "Marginal Utility" is the satisfaction derived from the last unit consumed. The "law of diminishing Marginal Utility" states that, after consuming a definite quantity of a good, or, for that matter, services, the marginal utility from it starts diminishing progressively as more and more units are added. What is demand? To put it simply, it is the quantity of a given good that a consumer is willing to purchase at different prices within a given period of time. However, it is guided by the following three factors. (1) Total income of the consumer (2) The prices of related goods, and, (3) Tastes. When the price of a good is increased -other things being equal - consumers will demand less and less of it. To put it in another way, if a particular good gets a larger supply i.e., more quantity is brought into the market, then - other things remaining constant - the good can only be sold at a lesser price. This is the basis of the Law of Downward Sloping Demand. Let us consider the Demand Schedule for a "T-shirt."

	Price $ (each)	Quantity Demanded (in thousands)
A	10	8
B	8	10
C	6	14
D	4	20
E	2	30

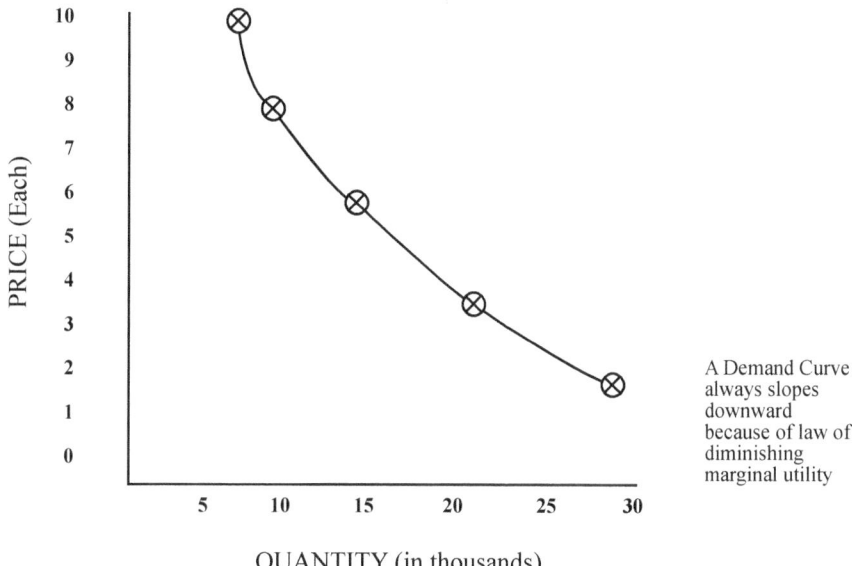

A Demand Curve always slopes downward because of law of diminishing marginal utility

The Law of Supply states that, other things being equal, an increase in the price of a good leads to an increase in the quantity supplied of it. The supply schedule or the supply curve depicts the relationship between market prices and the quantity of that good that producers are willing to supply. However, the supply curve is liable to shift depending on: (1) technological progress (2) change in import prices (3) change in taxes and duties (4) increase is the price of substitute goods in production (4) number of producers operating, and so on. Let us now consider the supply schedule for T-shirts.

	Price $ (each)	Quantity Supply (in thousands)
A	10	30
B	8	25
C	6	20
D	4	10
E	2	0

The Supply Curve Would Appear Like This:

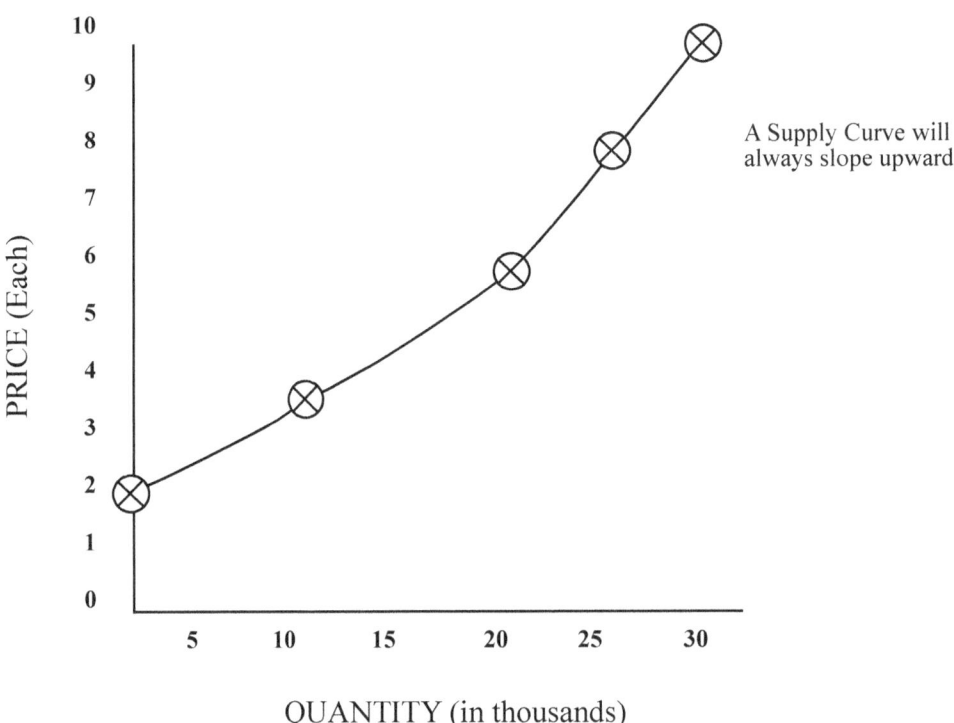

A Supply Curve will always slope upward

In a given market, if the consumers want more than what the producers are willing to supply, there is situation of **Excess Demand**. On the other side of the spectrum, if we have a market in which the supply by the producers is more than the demand by the consumers, there is bound to be an **Excess Supply**. If, in a situation where there is no excess demand, there is no excess supply. Then you have "market equilibrium." This can be represented graphically (let us consider our T-shirt illustrations on demand supply):

	Price $ (each)	Quantity Demanded (in thousands)	Quantity Supplied (in thousands)
A	10	8	30
B	8	10	25
C	6	14	20
D	4	20	10
E	2	30	0

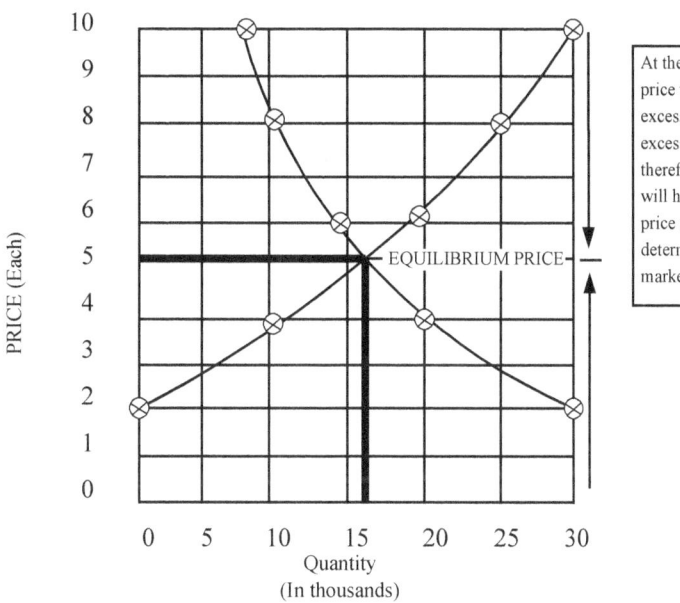

At the Equilibrium price there is no excess demand or excess supply and therefore that price will hold. This is how price and quantity are determined in the market.

CONSUMER DEMAND

A consumer is a citizen (an individual, a group of individuals, institutions) who consumes goods and services for the direct satisfaction of his or her desires or wants. Consumer behavior, therefore, is the way in which he or she chooses to spend his or her income.

Consumer's equilibrium refers to a state of mental satisfaction that a consumer feels is the maximum achievable for him under the given income and expenditure pattern. According to Paul A. Samuelson, the renowned economist, "…The consumer is in equi- librium when he maximizes his satisfaction given his income and the market prices..."

Utility is a yardstick for the satisfaction that a consumer derives from the consumption of goods and services.

Then what is total utility? Total utility is the sum total of satisfaction that a consumer derives from the consumption of all the units of a given commodity. Marginal utility, on the other hand, is the additional satisfaction that a consumer derives when he actually consumes one more unit of a given good.

Illustration:

Unit	Marginal Utility	Total Utility
First	15	15
Second	10	25
Third	5	30

Here Total Utility =$\sum$ Marginal Utility. In other words, Marginal Utility is the addition of a unit to the total utility by consuming one more unit of a given good.

Consumer Surplus refers to a situation where a given consumer's consumption of a particular unit is the actual difference between the maximum that the consumer would be willing to pay for that unit, and what he or she actually paid in the market. If a consumer buys a lot of units, then the consumer surplus on all such units bought is considered the total net benefit, in dollar terms, that the consumer gets from the purchase of each unit of the good at the market price.

DIMINISHING MARGINAL BENEFIT

This is closely related to the principle of diminishing marginal utility. The marginal benefit of a product/service tends to become lesser and lesser as more and more units are consumed.

Illustration:

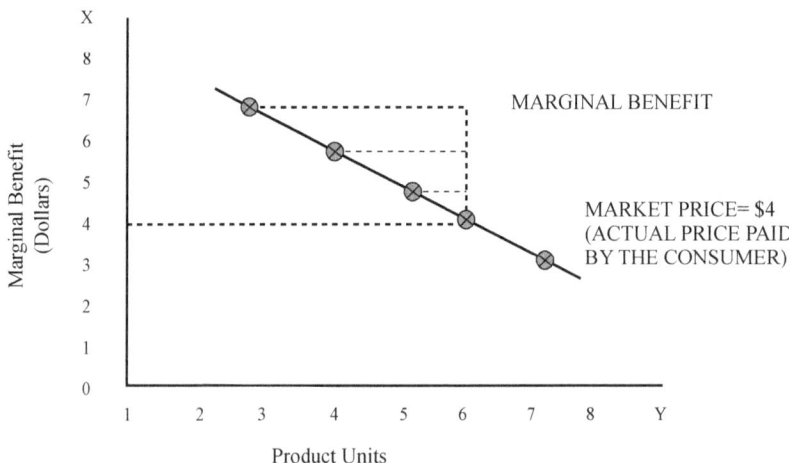

Here the consumer is willing to pay as much as $.7 to use this unit whereas the market price is only $.4 and therefore the consumer gets a psychological benefit of $.3 which is the marginal benefit for that unit. At $.3 he/she would definitely buy because that is less than the market price.

CONSUMER'S SURPLUS

This can be defined as the difference between the maximum price any given consumer would be willing to pay to obtain a given unit of good, and the amount actually paid in the market.

It is also a fact that the consumer surplus on all units of a given good purchased by a consumer is the Total Net Benefit that the consumer receives from being able to buy each unit of the good at market price.

Illustration:

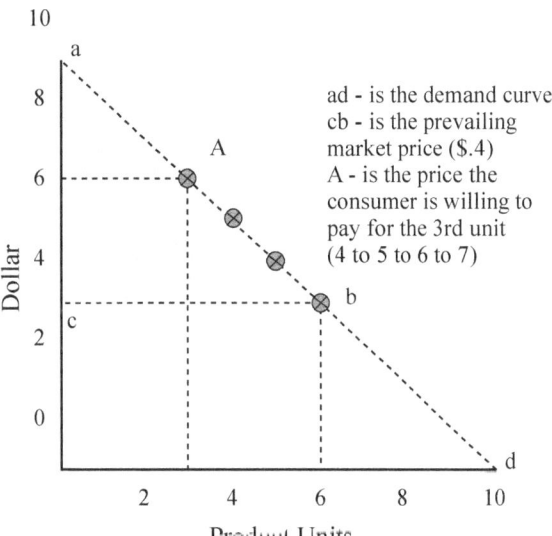

ad - is the demand curve
cb - is the prevailing market price ($.4)
A - is the price the consumer is willing to pay for the 3rd unit (4 to 5 to 6 to 7)

The consumer is willing to pay $.7 for the 3rd unit at point A even through the market price is $.4. The consumer, therefore, gets a psychological satisfaction of $.3 on the 3rd unit. The total consumer surplus on all units of product bought is given in the triangle abc, i.e., the shaded area.

The income line or price line or consumer budget line depicts different combinations of products that a consumer can obtain with an income of money under a set of ruling prices.

Principles of Microeconomics

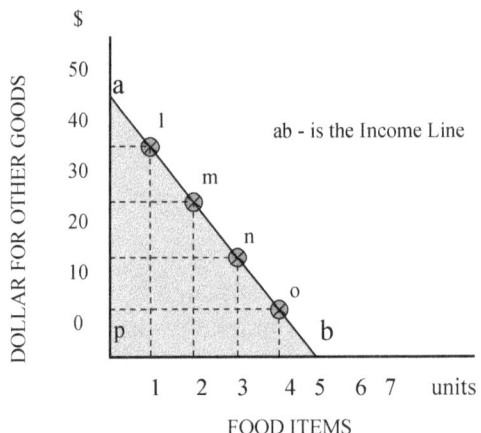

Each point on the line gives us the combination of essential food items, units and other goods from a to p that the consumer has a choice to buy. (He/She can buy either 50 dollars worth of other goods or 50 dollars worth of food items.) The consumer's Budget line has a constant slope, which means that at any point a, l, m, n, o, b, if the consumer buys an additional unit of food, he/she will have to go for 10 fewer units ($10.) of other goods. (The vertical distance ap ÷ the horizontal distance pb= 50÷5 =10.)

We now know that a consumer's demand curve is one that shows us different quantities of goods demanded by a consumer at different prices.

Illustration: <u>Consumer's Demand Curve</u>

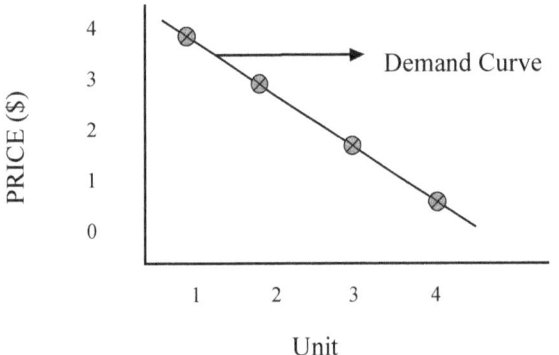

It shows the relationship between price and demand for a given consumer. When the price is $.1 the quantity demanded is 4 units. Likewise when the price is $.4 the quantity demanded is 1 unit.

Then, what is a Market Demand Curve? It is the curve that seeks to depict the total quantities of any given good demanded by all the consumers in a given market at different prices.

It can be referred to as the horizontal summation of the individual consumer's demand curve.

Market Demand Curve as Summation of Individual Consumer Demand Curve

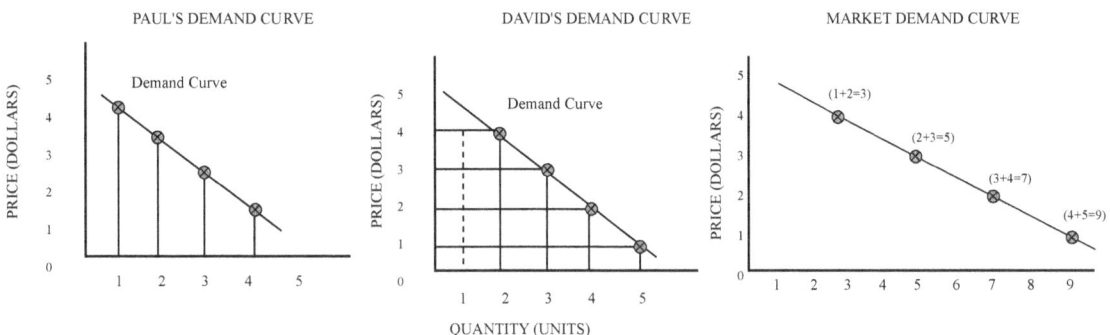

Market Demand

Paul's 1 + David's 2 = 3
Paul's 2 + David's 3 = 5
Paul's 3 + David's 4 = 7
Paul's 4 + David's 5 = 9

SHIFT IN DEMAND CURVE

Demand tends to extend or contract depending upon whether there is a decrease or increase in the price of a given commodity.

Illustration:

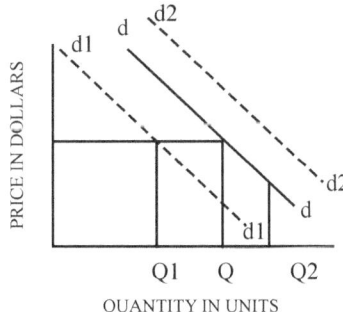

An increase in demand shifts the 'dd' Curve rightward to d2d2. A decrease in demand shifts the 'dd' Curve leftward to d1d1.

dd - is the normal demand Curve
d2d2 - is the demand curve shifted to right because of increase in demand.
d1d1 - is the demand curve shifted leftward on account of a decrease in demand.

Likewise, if there is an increase or decrease in the income of consumers, how will it affect the Demand Curve? Let us assume that other things remain constant. How will increase/decrease of consumer's income affect 'dd' Curve?

Principles of Microeconomics

Illustration:

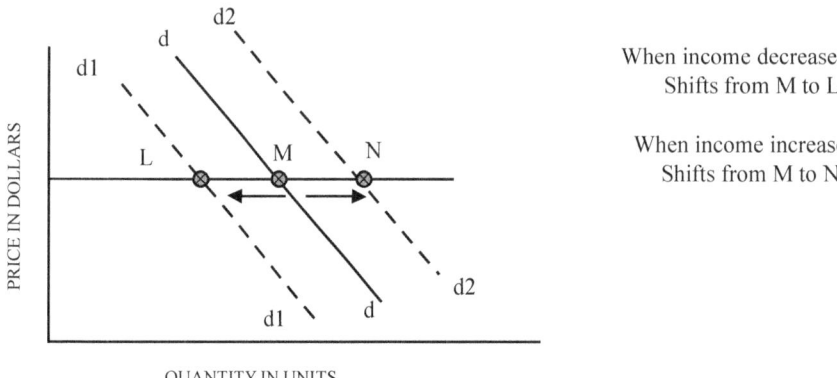

When income decreases Shifts from M to L.

When income increase Shifts from M to N.

ELASTICITY OF DEMAND

According to Marshall: "…Elasticity of Demand may be defined as the percentage change in the quantity demanded divided by the percentage change in the price…" Of the three Elasticities available, viz., (1) Price Elasticity of Demand (2) Income Elasticity of Demand and, (3) Cross Elasticity of Demand, we will concentrate only on Price Elasticity of Demand.

Percentage of change in demand divided by the percentage change in price is, as we know from Marshall's definition, the Price Elasticity of Demand. There are 3 methods by which Price Elasticity is measured:

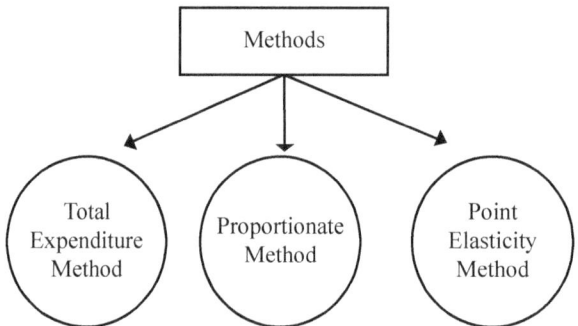

Of these, the total expenditure method will suffice for this level of study. Total expenditure method was evolved by Marshall. In this method there are 3 possible situations.

Situation 1:

Price of Goods (Dollars)	Quantity in units	Total expenditure in Dollar terms	Effect on the Expenditure	Basicity of Demand
2	4	8	No Change	Unitary i.e. $E_d = 1$
1	8	8		

Situation 2:

Price of Goods ($)	Quantity in Units	Total Expenditure in Dollar terms	Effect on Total expenditure	Elasticity of Demand
2	4	8	Increased expenditure	Greater than Unity. $E_d > 1$
1	10	10		

Situation 3:

Price of Goods ($)	Quantity in Units	Total Expenditure in Dollar terms	Effect on Total expenditure	Elasticity of Demand
2	3	6	Decreased expenditure	Less than Unity. $E_d < 1$
1	4	4		

Graphically it can be shown as below.

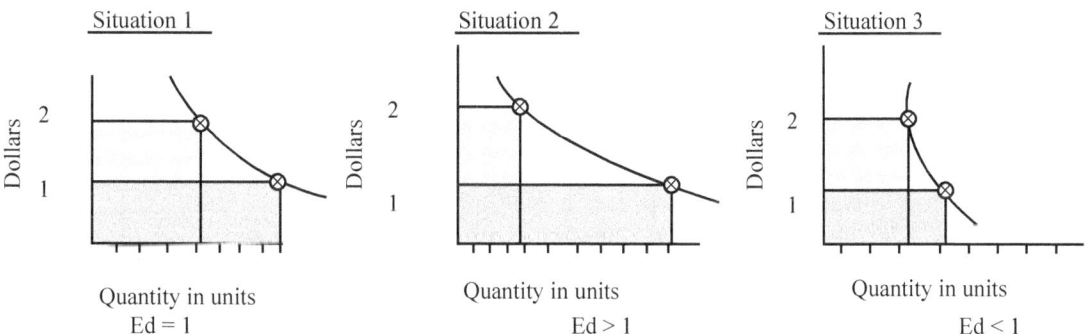

FIRM'S PRODUCTION COST AND REVENUE

Firms turn out outputs. Outputs require inputs for value addition. For production of goods and services, one requires land, labor, and capital as inputs. The relationship between physical inputs and physical outputs is known as 'Production Function' in economics.

Marginal Product and Diminishing Returns

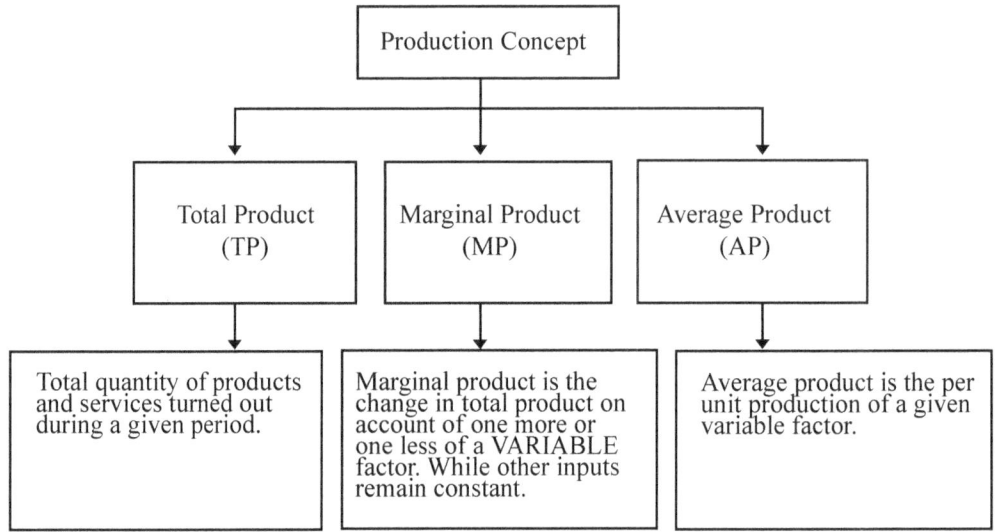

If more units of one input are added, the marginal product of the variable input should necessarily decline. Here the assumption is that all other inputs are held constant.

Prof. Beham has put it succinctly: "…as the proportion of one factor in a combination of factors is increased, after a point, the marginal product of that factor will diminish…."

Illustration:

Total and Marginal Product Curves

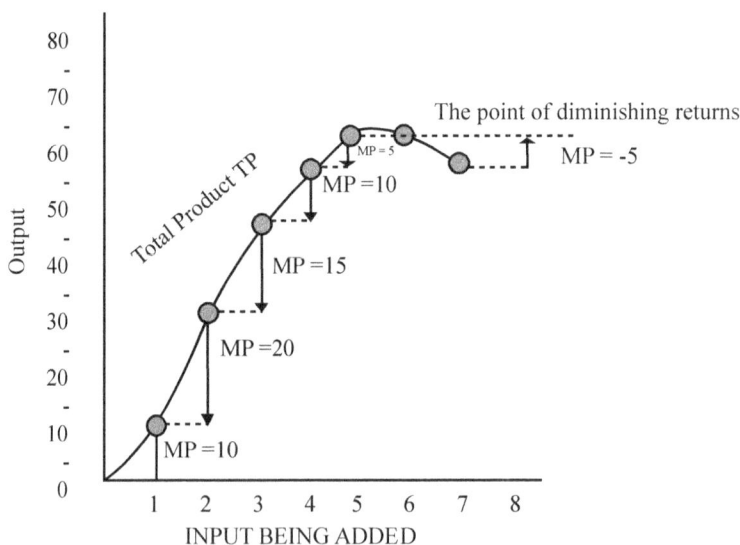

Total, Average, Marginal Costs, and Revenue

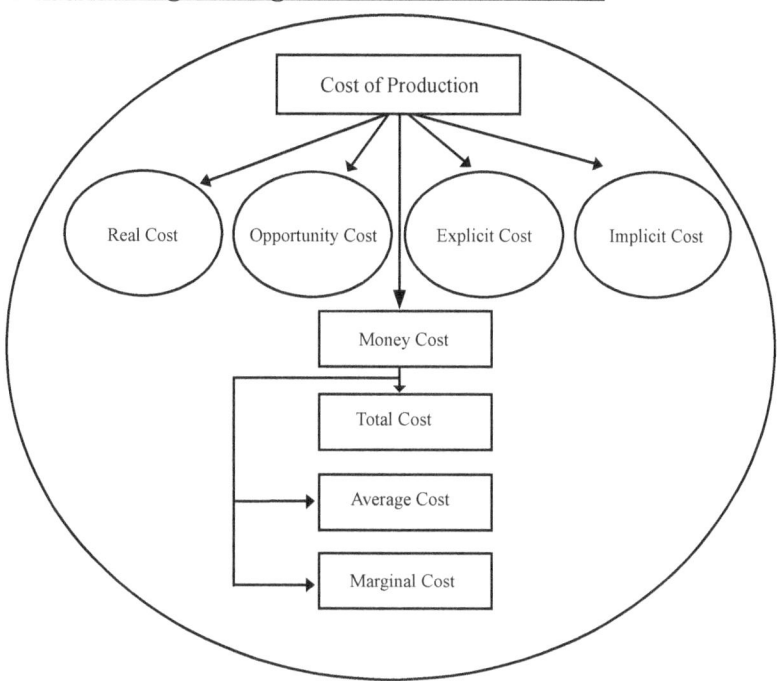

Real Cost:
Has no monetary effect; it is more in terms of mental and physical efforts put in and sacrifices suffered in the production of the commodity.

Opportunity Cost:
Refers to the opportunity foregone in terms of the next foremost alternative utilization of the factor.

Explicit Cost:
Cash payments made by the firm to outside sources for using their goods and services.

Implicit Cost:
According to Leftwitch; "…implicit costs are costs of self-owned and self-employed resources…."

Money Cost:
It is the sum total of payments made to all factors of production in producing the product.

Principles of Microeconomics

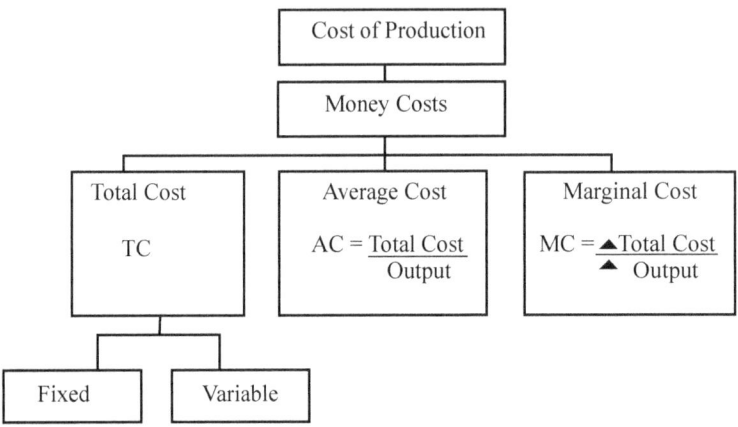

Total Cost:

It is the sum total of all expenses incurred in order to produce a given volume of output. It has two components (1) Fixed costs, and (2) Variable costs. Fixed costs do not change with the change in output, i.e., whether a firm produces one unit or ten units, fc remains the same.

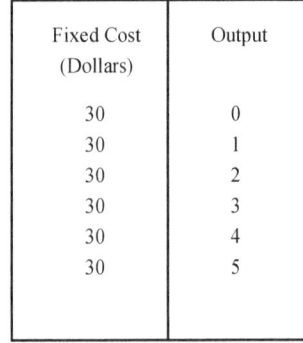
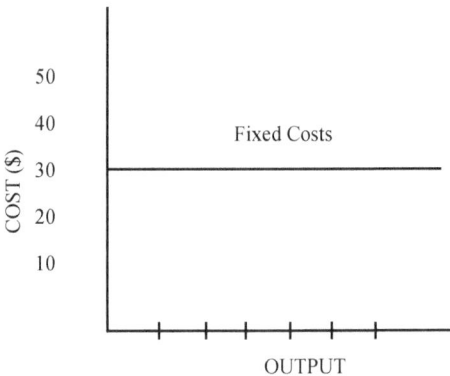

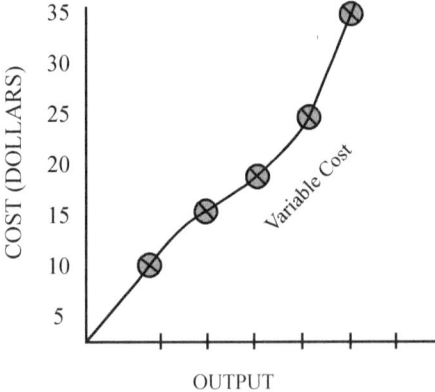

Variable Costs $	Output
0	0
10	1
15	2
18	3
25	4
35	5

Average cost (AC) (aka) Average Total Cost (ATC) is arrived at by dividing the total cost (TC) by number of units manufactured. To put it in another way, AC = average Fixed Costs (AFC) + average variable cost (AVC). AC= AFC+AVC.

Marginal Cost:
Ferguson states: "…Marginal Cost is the addition to the total cost due to the addition of one unit of output…" That is to say that MC is the increase in TC when one additional or extra unit is manufactured.

Illustration:

Output	Fixed Cost $	Variable Cost $	Total Cost $	Marginal Cost $
0	30	0	30	--
1	30	10	40	10
2	30	15	45	5
3	30	18	48	3
4	30	25	55	7
5	30	35	65	10

Graphically shown it would look like:

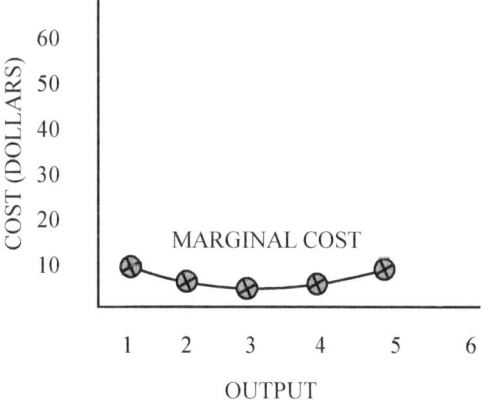

Marginal Cost is arrived at by measuring the difference between the total cost factors of two units.

REVENUE

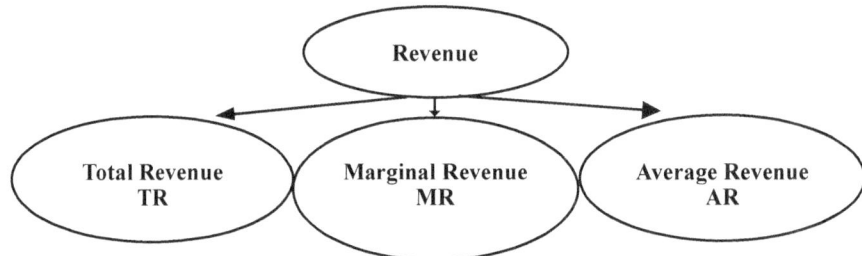

What is Revenue? Firms produce goods for the sake of selling them to the consumers (of course at a profit).

Whatever the proceeds, in money terms, a firm receives on such selling is known as the revenue of the firm.

While total revenue is the sum total of all sale income of a given firm, Marginal Revenue is the change in the total revenue (income) arising out of one more or one less unit of output. Average revenue is the income received from the sale of a product on per unit basis. MR is calculated by a few equations in economics. They are:

(1) $MR = \dfrac{\text{Change in Total Revenue}}{\text{Change in Units Sold}} = \dfrac{\blacktriangle TR}{\blacktriangle U}$

It can also be stated that MR=TRn-TRn-1, where

(2)   TRn= Total Revenue of 'n' units sold and TRn-1=Total Revenue of n-1 units.

Example:

Let us say that the total revenue = $2000 when 20 units of a product are sold. Suppose if the TR increases to $2200 when the 21st unit of the product is sold, then the firm realizes additional revenue of $200 on account of the sale of an addition unit.

(2) $MR = TR_n - TR_{n-1}$
         $= \$2200 - \$2000 = \$200$

If we use the other equation $\dfrac{\blacktriangle TR}{\blacktriangle U}$

Method (1): MR = $\frac{\Delta TR}{\Delta U}$

$$MR = \frac{2200 - 2000}{21 - 20} = \frac{200}{1}$$

MR = $200

TR, MR & AR – An Illustration

Output	PRICE (Average Revenue)	Total	Marginal Revenue $
1	100	100	100
2	80	160	60 (160 - 100)
4	40	160	0 (160 - 160)
5	30	150	-10 (150 - 160)

Graphically, the relationship between TR, AR and MR can be illustrated as below:

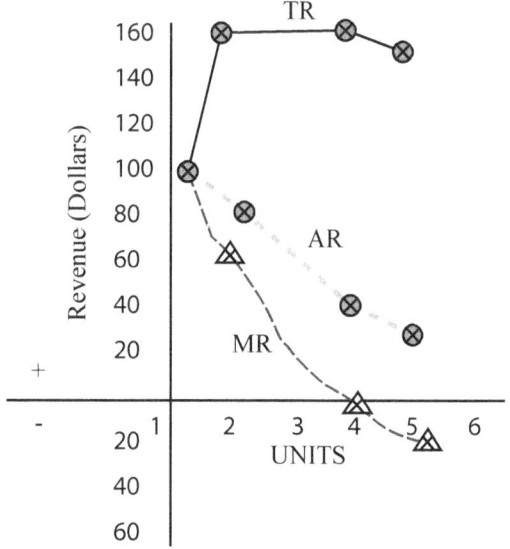

LONG RUN COSTS AND ECONOMIES OF SCALE

In the long run, all factors are bound to become variable, as there won't be any perceptible difference or distinction between variable costs and fixed costs. Always, the long period total cost curve originates from zero - which is the beginning – mainly because in the long run all costs tend to become variable costs as they vary according to output. At zero; variable costs also become zero.

LONG PERIOD TOTAL COST CURVES

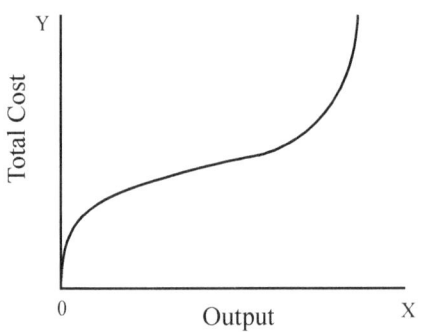

- Starts from zero
- Increases at a slow rate initially
- Then reaches constancy for a while
- Finally thrusts itself at a higher rate of increase

- Normally, long run cost curves are found to be flatter than short period cost curves. It is mainly because of a firm's expansion plans – i.e., adding more machines. Also it is possible that the firm shifts from one scale of production to another. In a short run it is not workable.
- Long period AC and MC cost curves are always "U" shaped mainly because of economies and diseconomies of scale. It happens because of LAC's tendency to decline in answer to economies of scale. It rises in response to diseconomies of scale. It reaches a state of constancy in a situation where economies of scale bal- ance diseconomies of scale. Graphically;

Long Period Average – AC - and Marginal Cost – MC - Curves:

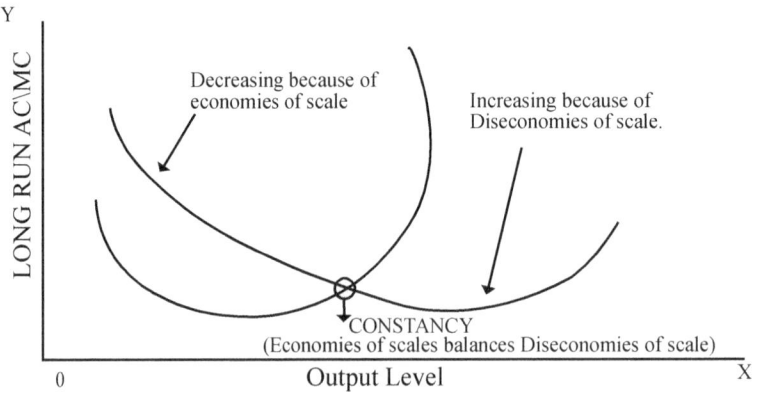

ECONOMIES OF SCALE

An increase in scale of operation means an increase in all the factors in the same degree and at the same time. If all inputs are quadrupled, then the output tends to be more than quadrupled. This phenomenon is known as "increasing return to scale." According to Watson, "…Returns to scale relates to the behavior of total output as all inputs are varied in same proportion and it is a long run concept…"

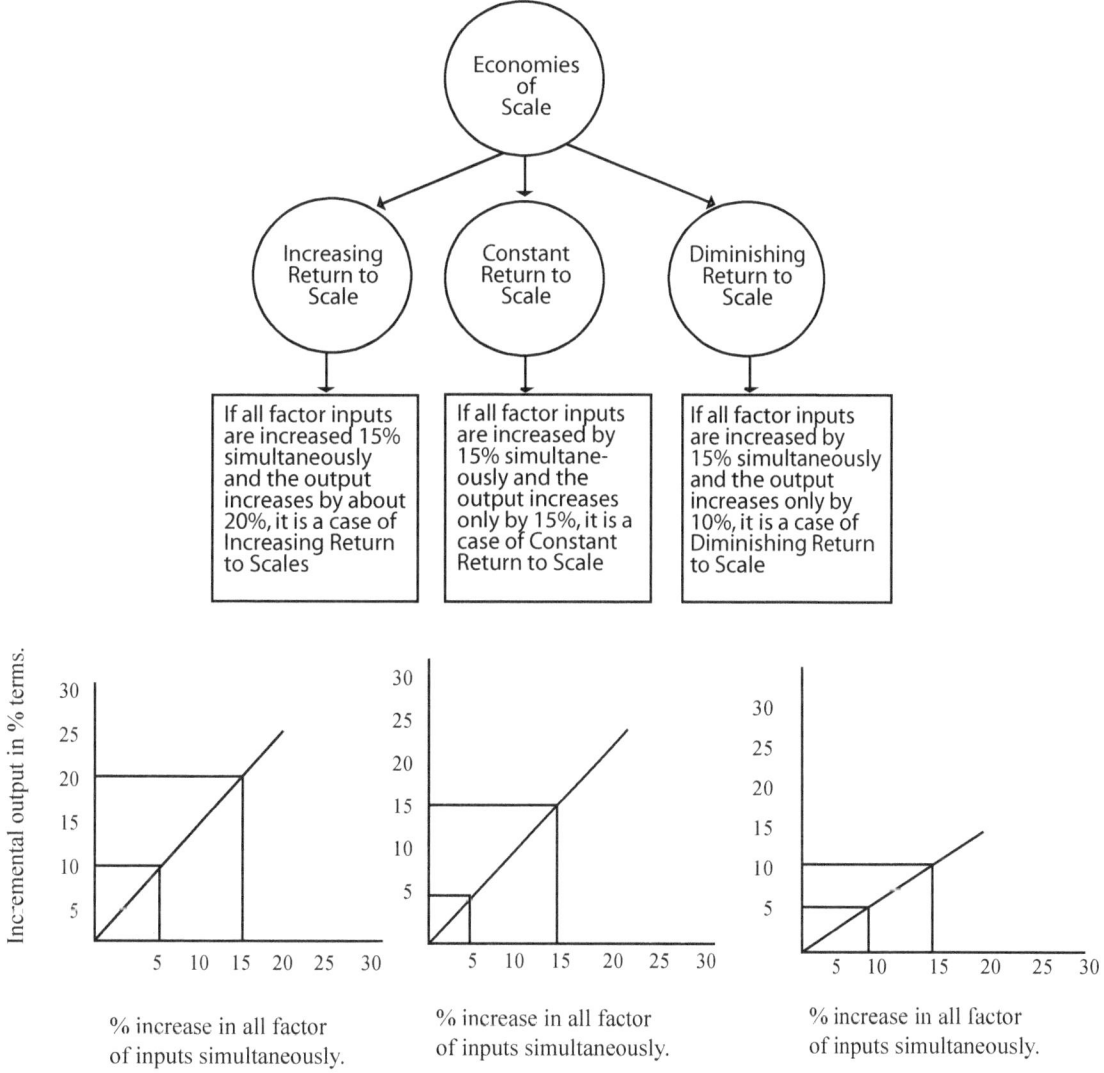

Increasing returns to scale reduces unit cost of production or increases output per unit of factor inputs employed.

Principles of Microeconomics

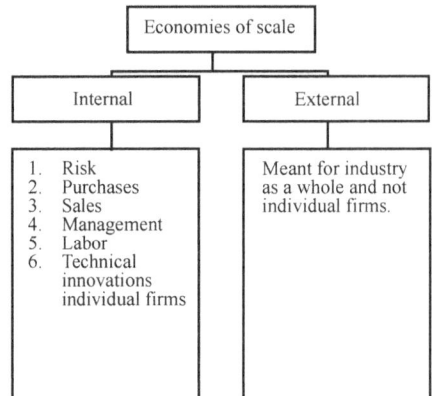

PROFIT MAXIMIZATION: PRICING, REVENUE AND OUTPUT BOTH IN THE LONG RUN AND THE SHORT RUN AND IN THE FIRM AND THE MARKET

PERFECT COMPETITION

Under perfect competition any given industry's equilibrium rests where "market supply" = "market demand."

The firms within the industry accept as "price line" where market supply and market demand balance each other.

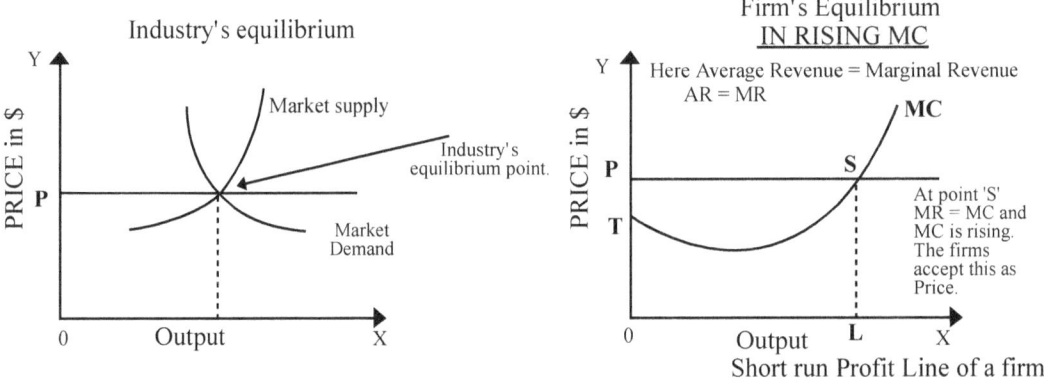

Under perfect competition, let us see the long run equilibrium of a given firm:

Illustration:

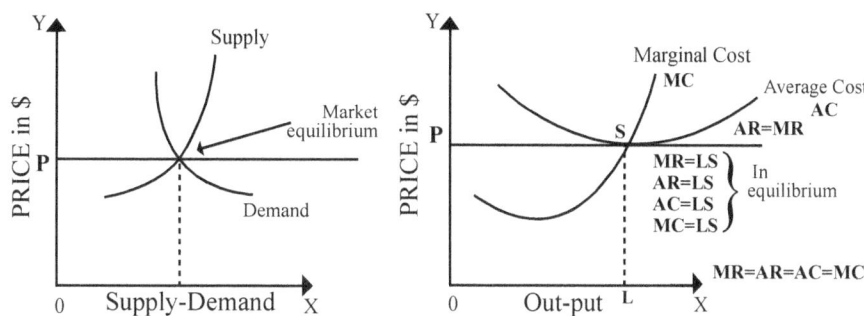

- This is long run equilibrium of a given firm. The firm attempts to get only normal profits (AR=AC).
- As in the short period, here also the industry's equilibrium price determined at the point where the market supply meets the market demand is taken as the price by the firm.
- Gross profit of given firm can be maximized only if the Price=MC. (Gross Profit=Total Revenue TR-Total Variable Cost TVC. Price=AR.) In perfect com- petition AR=MR because the firm's price is nothing but the industry's equilibrium price. Profit Maximization, therefore, occurs when marginal revenue=marginal cost MR=MC.
- Price under perfect competition is decided by the industry. No individual firm can have a say in its pricing. Likewise firms belonging to an industry cannot change the equilibrium price as it is set by the market, under perfect competition.
- Differences between perfect competition, monopolistic competition and monopoly are given below.

    Perfect competition
    Large number of buyers and sellers of a given homogenous good.
    Monopolistic
    Large number of buyers and sellers of a differentiated product.
    Monopoly
    Large number of buyers but only one seller.
- Under Perfect competition the seller has no control over price
- Under Monopolistic competition the seller has partial control over price
- Under Monopoly, the price is what the supplier demands
- We know that in the case of perfect competition AR=MR. In the case of monopolistic competition and monopoly, it is always AR>MR.

MONOPOLISTIC COMPETITION

The difference between monopolistic competition and monopoly is that the AR and MR curves are more realistic in the former. In the case of monopolistic competition, if the price is raised, demand will fall and the fall in demand will be proportionately more. Product differentiations are the watchwords for monopolistic competition. If the price of "Colgate" toothpaste is raised, there are other brands, like "Forhans," "Mcleans" and many others with slight differentiation, which can be bought, so the price rise will have a more than proportionate decrease in demand. Substitution is the name of the game under monopolistic competition.

MONOPOLY

In this setup, if there is a price increase, the demand will definitely fall, but fall almost in proportion to the increase. Price rise will fetch lesser units of output. Decrease in price will fetch more units of output. The revenue curves =AR and MR- are bound to slope downwards under perfect competition; 'AR' is what the market decides. In other words 'AR' is not what the firm sets but is decided by the supply and demand equilibrium of the market. Under perfect competition, therefore, AR is represented always by a horizontal line. Let us now study graphically demand curves price line of different market conditions.

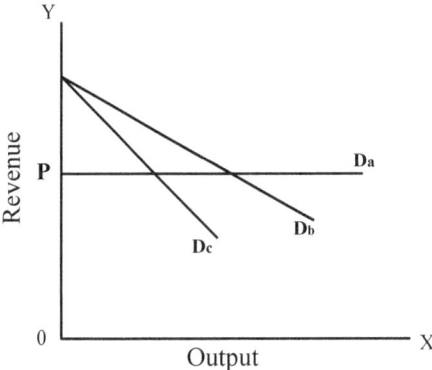

We know that the demand curve, i.e., the price line of a given firm is the same as the AR curve of that firm.

Da is the AR, i.e., the price line under perfect competition.
Db is the AR, i.e., the price line under monopolistic competition. Dc is the AR, i.e., the price line under monopoly competition.

Oligopoly is a market situation where there are a very limited number of sellers, who trade in differentiated or standardized products. An oligopoly comes into being only when there are a few sellers who dominate the market as against only one seller in the case of monopoly.

EFFICIENCY

Productive performance at its best is efficiency. If we utilize all the resources most productively we get efficiency. In other words, efficiency is the objective of getting the maximum out of our productive efforts. There is (a) allocative efficiency and (b) technological efficiency. If we are able to produce a best possible mix of goods and services utilizing relevant resources, or, inputs at the best possible cost, i.e., at the lowest cost possible, we have allocative efficiency. On the other hand if we are in a position to thwart wasted efforts at every step of resource, or input utilization on the one hand, and, more importantly, be able to thwart lax, sloppy and disorderly management on the other, we have technological efficiency.

Government, on its part, tries its best to offer a level playing field for all entrepreneurs by enacting laws and regulations. The government regulation of business can be:

(a) To prevent collusion between firms to dry up competition.
(b) To protect the quality of resources like water and air, enact environmental regula- tions.
(c) To protect the quality of health, safety and working conditions, enact proper regu- lations.
(d) Regulatory controls on any industry's price, conditions of entry, etc.

The anti-trust law (a.k.a. competition act or anti-combines law) seeks to nullify different strategies and tactics, as business firms spring up from time to time, to lessen or totally nullify competition in an industry by prescribing stringent penalties on those who dare to break the rules and regulations.

Factor Market

DERIVED DEMAND

Let us take, say, bread. Bread is the product available in the market. Flour is a major input of bread. The demand for flour is entirely dependent on the demand for the end-product, viz., bread. If the demand for an input item depends mainly on the demand for the end product of which it is part and parcel, it is a case of derived demand.

According to Paul A. Samuelson, one of America's great economists, "…Derived Demand refers to the fact that, when profit-seeking firms demand a factor of production, they do so because that factor input permits them to produce a good which consumers are willing to pay for now or in the future. The demand for the factor of production is thus derived ultimately from consumer's desires and demands for final goods…"

DETERMINATION OF WAGES AND OTHER FACTORS OF PRODUCTION

We produce goods by employing such inputs as land, labor and capital. Land and labor are often called "primary factors of production." Capital in economics is mostly referring to capital goods. Paul A. Samuelson says: "…Capital goods, then, represent produced goods that can be used as factor inputs for further production, whereas labor and land are primary factor inputs not usefully thought of as being themselves produced by the economic system…."

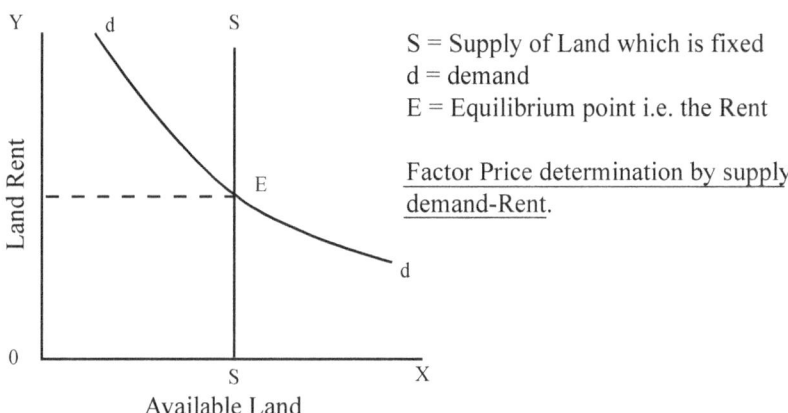

S = Supply of Land which is fixed
d = demand
E = Equilibrium point i.e. the Rent

Factor Price determination by supply demand-Rent.

In a competitive equilibrium, if the skills and mental efficiencies of all work on the one hand, men and the job requirements on the other are homogenous, i.e., all workmen are equally skilled and the job demands are identical, there would not be any wage differentials. The wage rate would necessarily be determined at the equilibrium point of labor supply and demand. However, individuals are distinctly different in skills, acumen and dexterity. Naturally, a person who uses better productive methods demands a much higher wage rate than another less skilled worker.

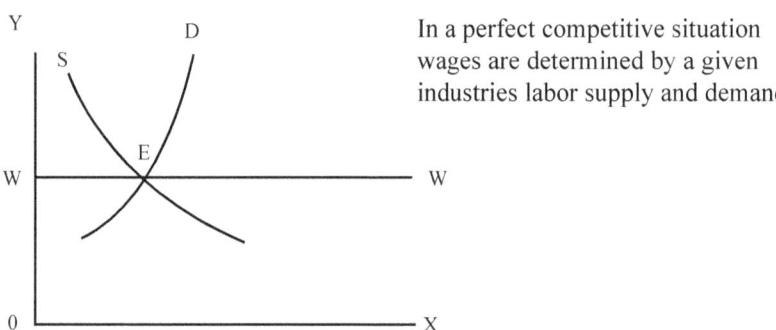

In a perfect competitive situation wages are determined by a given industries labor supply and demand.

DISTRIBUTION OF INCOME

The American standard of living is one of the best in the world. Why? It is income! The per capita income of an American is, again, one of the best in the world.

Let us study what Warren J. Keegan, in his wonderful book on international marketing "Global Marketing Management" says: "…The U.S. market, with per capita income of $25,000, over $6 trillion in 1993 income, and a population of over 250 million people is enormous. Other industrialized countries with similar per capita income are nevertheless quite small in terms of total annual income. In Sweden, for example, per capita GNP is 26,300; Sweden's smaller population of only 8.4 million means that annual income is only about $227 billion. About 75% of the world's GNP is located in the triad - North America, Japan, and Western Europe…"

Income is an important factor in an individual's life. The more the disposable income at one's command, the more the standard of living. Even countries are segmented on the basis of distribution of income.

High Income Countries - $ 12,000 Plus
Upper Middle Income Countries - $ 2,000 Plus Lower Middle income Countries - $ 400 Plus Low income Countries - $ <400

Every occupation demands income according to the risks involved, educational background and training needed, and, of course, against supply and demand.

In every society inequalities do exist.

Market Failures and the Role of Government

EXTERNALITIES, PUBLIC GOOD AND INFORMATION ECONOMICS

EXTERNALITIES: A.K.A. SPILLOVER OR THIRD PARTY EFFECT

- Externalities:
  It can be defined as either a detrimental or a beneficial side effect of supply and demand, i.e., production and consumption that occur in a given economy. Example: if you inoculate your child against small pox, you are not only ensuring that your child does not suffer this dreaded disease in his/her lifetime but, on the external plane, you are ensuring your child will not be the one who spreads the disease to other children in the neighborhood. Externalities affect people

or businesses who remain outside the producer-consumer continuum. An externality may have a beneficial effect (vaccination) or create a negative effect (pollution) on society. Governments all over the world always try to encourage actions that are deemed to create external benefits to the economy. By the same token, they try their best always to curb actions that are deemed to create negative externalities.

- Governments always ensure that the consumers consume only the goods that are not harmful. They restrict or prohibit goods that are harmful and known to affect a negative externality such as tobacco, cigarettes, drugs, etc.
- Governments all over the world do their best to bridge the gap of inequality between rich and poor by bringing in legislation to protect the poor by formulating meaningful programs.
- Every government tries its best to maintain economic stability so that the subjects are assured of continued income. Then they tax the subjects in order to program beneficial externalities.
- Governments seek to provide public goods themselves, as no private business would think of it as it does not reap enough incentives.

In the words of Paul A. Samuelson, the American economist who has given to posterity "Economics," a magnum opus in its own right and considered by many as the Bible of economics, "…An 'external economy' is defined as a favorable effect on one or more persons that emanates from the action of a different person or firm; it shifts the cost or utility curve of each person it helps, and such an externally caused shift should be distinguished from any internal movement along the affected individual's own cost curve.

An 'external diseconomy' is defined in the same way, except that it refers to external harm that is done to others. The case where expansion of fishing by others in limited waters serves to shift up each boat's cost curves would be an example of an external diseconomy; another case would be one where each man's haste to drill for oil near his neighbors' boundaries lowers the amount of oil ever recovered. Smoke nuisance and water pollution are two familiar other instances…"

PUBLIC GOOD

It is the good or service that has enormous benefits for society and which has got to be provided willy-nilly irrespective of who pays. We can cite the case of governments shooting up very expensive weather satellites up above the globe and keeping them at geo-stationary orbit for tracking weather. Is it necessary? Well it is. Countries need rain so that they can plan ploughing operations well in advance for their arable lands. Weather has vagaries, which cannot be predicted by just looking at the sky. Weather satellites send in most informative and really meaningful data about the behavior of weather in a given segment of the earth from which it is easy to arrive at the time and duration of a wet spell or a dry spell. It, therefore, is a public good that no individual businessmen will venture, not because he cannot do it, but because of a lack of sufficient incentive. Considering the society as a whole - in fact the country as a whole - the government of the day has to provide such services in the larger interests of the people.

Pollution-free air available to you on account of the government's anti-pollution programs after meeting huge expenses still comes to you free. You enjoy your morning walk. However, if you want to see the latest movie, you have to pay for it because it is a private good/service. A private good or service never comes free but most of the public goods or services are. This principle is known as exclusion principle. It is the basis for knowing or noticing, or distinguishing, which is a public good and which is a private good (or non-public good). If people from a given economy are excluded from enjoying a good unless they pay for it, it is not a public good.

Building a dam, paving roads, generation of electricity, having an efficient police system or providing an excellent national defense system, safety and health, controlling pollution, - these are meant to be public goods; governments, in the larger interests of their subjects provide them without charging anything.

Economics is a very vital part of any functioning government. Information and data are essential for economic decisions. Statistics provide a basic structure for economic programming.

Information gathering has been extremely difficult in earlier times. Today, with the advent of information technology, we have a veritable information explosion amidst us. When hunting for information and data, we are now in the happy situation of choosing from a sea of information and data.

Graphs To Know

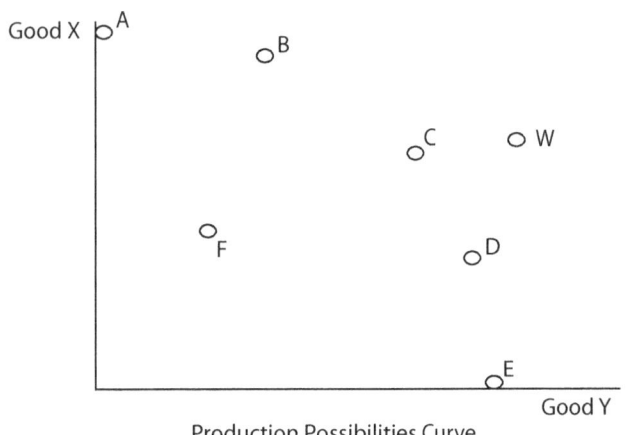
Production Possibilities Curve

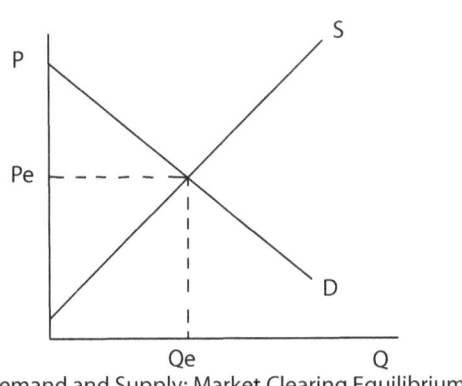
Demand and Supply: Market Clearing Equilibrium

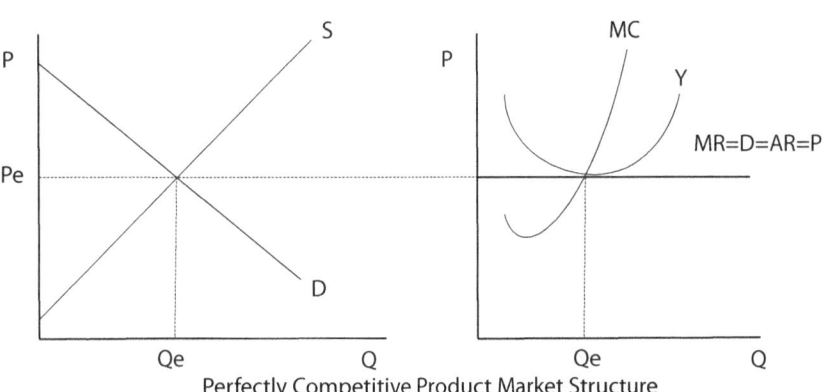
Perfectly Competitive Product Market Structure

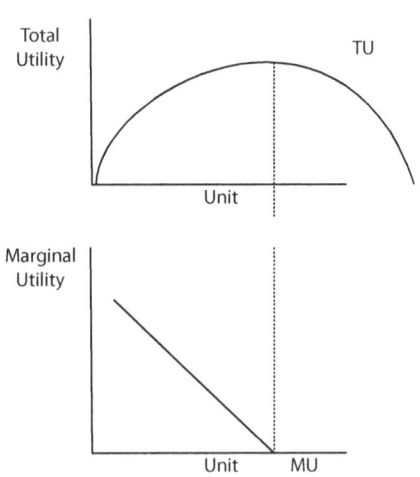

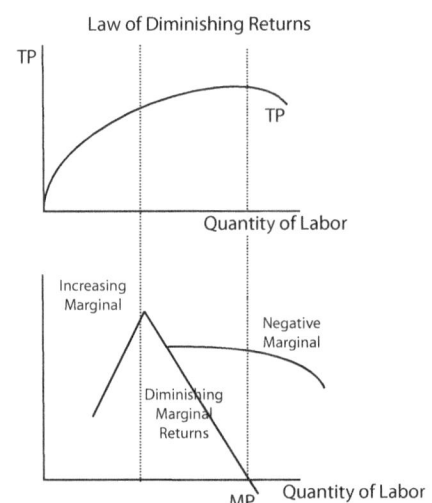

Principles of Microeconomics

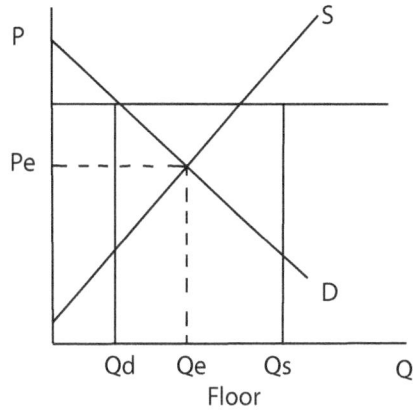
Floor

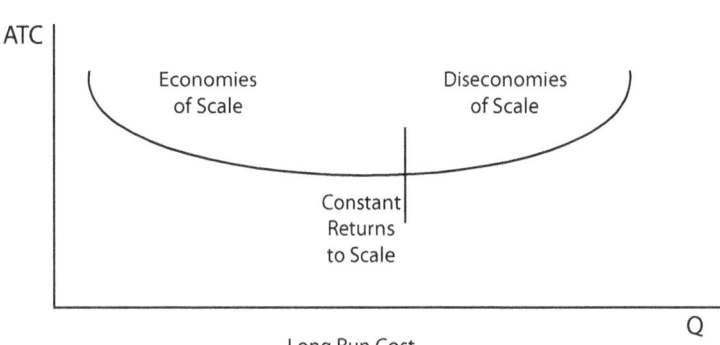
Long Run Cost

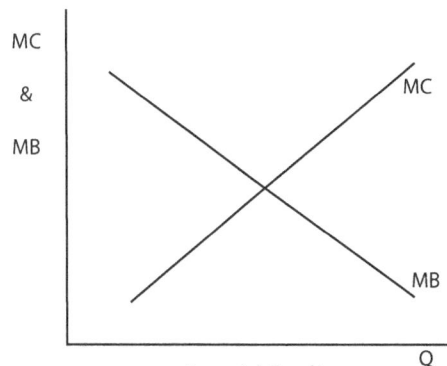
Essential Graph

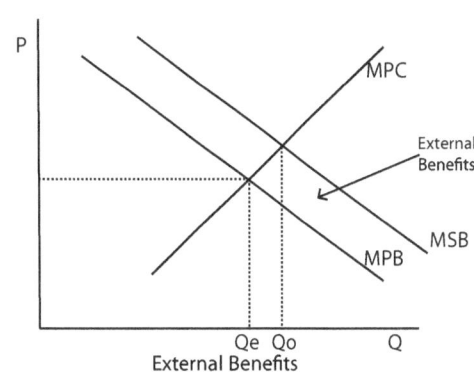
External Benefits

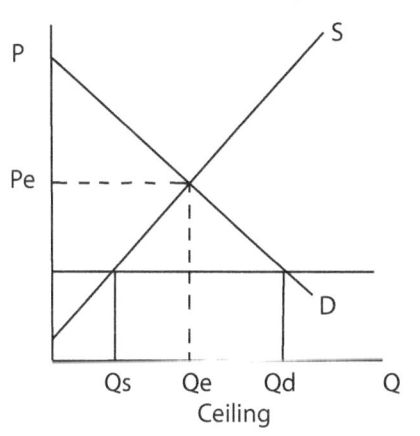
Ceiling

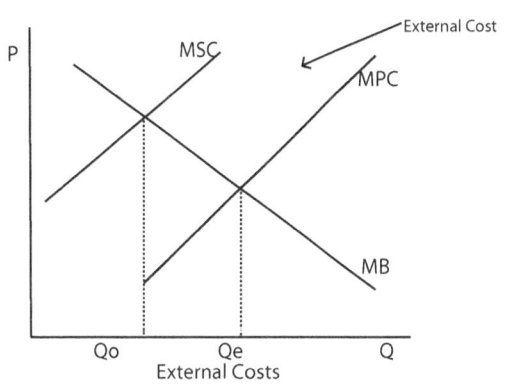
External Costs

Sample Test Questions

1) Scarcity forces choices to be decided about the use of

   A) Supply and demand
   B) People and prices
   C) Workforce, workplace and management
   D) Money and goods
   E) Land, labor and capital

The correct answer is E:) Land labor and capital. When scarcity exists, choices must be made about the use of land, labor and capital.

2) Zero economic profit in the long run applies only to

   A) Monopolistic Competition Markets
   B) Oligopolies
   C) Monopolies
   D) Pure competition markets
   E) All of the above

The correct answer is D:) Pure competition markets.

3) The production possibilities curve's main purpose is to

   A) Show current production
   B) Make choices
   C) Increase production
   D) Detail incoming resources
   E) Illustrate inefficiency in production

The correct answer is B:) Make choices. A production possibilities curve shows the possible allocation of resources allowing choices to be made in how to use them.

4) The price for a pizza goes up from 10 dollars to 12 dollars and sales for pizzas decrease. Because the sales for pizza decrease, the demand for soda also decreases. If the demand for soda decreases by 12%, what is the cross price elasticity of demand?

   A) -6
   B) -1.7
   C) -0.6
   D) 0.6
   E) 1.7

The correct answer is C:) -0.6. The pizza increased in price by 20%, and the demand decreased by 12%. Using the formula (-12%)/20% the answer is -.06.

5) The author of the theory of comparative advantage is

   A) Denis Robertson
   B) James Tobin
   C) David Ricardo
   D) Stephan Nickell
   E) Milton Freedman

The correct answer is C:) David Ricardo. David Ricardo is the author of the theory of comparative advantage.

6) Which of the following is the correct formula for cross price inelasticity of demand between two products?

   A) Cross Price Elasticity of Demand $= \dfrac{\text{Percent change in the Demand for Product 2}}{\text{Percent change in the Price of Product 1}}$

   B) Cross Price Elasticity of Demand $= \dfrac{\text{Percent change in the Demand for Product 1}}{\text{Percent change in the Price of Product 2}}$

   C) Cross Price Elasticity of Demand $= \dfrac{\text{Percent change in the Demand for Product 2}}{\text{Percent change in the Supply of Product 1}}$

   D) Cross Price Elasticity of Demand $= \dfrac{\text{Percent change in the Price for Product 2}}{\text{Percent change in the Demand of Product 1}}$

   E) Cross Price Elasticity of Demand $= \dfrac{\text{Percent change in the Price for Product 1}}{\text{Percent change in the Demand of Product 2}}$

The correct answer is A:)

Cross Price Elasticity of Demand $= \dfrac{\text{Percent change in the Demand for Product 2}}{\text{Percent change in the Price of Product 1}}$

7) Who or what decides how an economy is run in a command economy?

   A) The central government
   B) A small group of individuals
   C) The people
   D) Supply and demand
   E) Customs and rituals

The correct answer is A:) The central government. In a command economy, the essential questions of how to run the economy are decided by the central government.

8) A cartel would most likely form in a market that is a(n)

   A) Oligopoly
   B) Monopoly
   C) Monopolistic competition
   D) Pure competition
   E) Any of the above

The correct answer is A:) Oligopoly. A cartel is a grouping of a few large powerful entities, which is what exists in an oligopoly.

9) An essential work incentive to the very poor of a given society is

   A) Food stamps
   B) Retirement
   C) 401k
   D) Wage subsidy
   E) None of the above

The correct answer is D:) Wage subsidy.

10) Which of the following is NOT an example of a price ceiling?

   A) The government creates a new law setting the maximum price of flour at 10 dollars a pound.
   B) A principle makes a new rule setting the maximum price of school shirts at 15 dollars.
   C) The government creates regulations which limit the maximum price of rent.
   D) The government creates laws setting a minimum wage which employees can be paid.
   E) Both B and D

The correct answer is E:) Both B and D. B is not a price ceiling because they must be set by the government, and D is a price floor, not price ceiling.

11) When a surplus exists in the market it means

   A) The price is below the equilibrium
   B) The price is above the equilibrium
   C) The price is at the equilibrium
   D) The quantity is at the equilibrium
   E) The quantity is below the equilibrium

The correct answer is B:) The price is above the equilibrium.

12) Which type of market is in a state of Nash equilibrium?

   A) Oligopoly
   B) Pure competition
   C) Labor
   D) Monopoly
   E) Monopolistic competition

The correct answer is A:) Oligopoly. Oligopolies have many large companies who monitor and react to each other's actions. Nash equilibrium is when groups or people make the best decisions they can based on the decisions others make.

13) The Law of Supply stares that

   A) As prices increase, demand decreases
   B) As prices increase, demand increases
   C) As prices increase, demand remains the same
   D) As prices decrease, demand decreases
   E) As prices decrease, demand remains the same

The correct answer is A:) As prices increase, demand decreases. The Law of Supply states that as the price of a certain good increases, the demand for that good or service diminishes.

14) A company is trying to decide which of its employees to assign the unimportant task of filing papers. They know that one employee, Melissa, can file 20 papers an hour and help 5 important customers in an hour. Another employee, George, can file 18 papers in an hour and help 2 important customers. Who has the com- parative advantage for filing papers?

   A) Melissa because she is faster at filing papers.
   B) George because he is faster at filing papers.
   C) Melissa because she has a higher opportunity cost.
   D) George because he has a lower opportunity cost.
   E) Cannot be determined without more information.

The correct answer is D:) George because he has a lower opportunity cost. The person with the lower opportunity cost has the higher comparative advantage. The company chooses George with the opportunity cost of slightly slower filing, instead of Melissa with the opportunity cost of many fewer important customers helped.

15) An improvement in production technology for a certain good leads to

   A) An increase in demand for the good
   B) An increase in supply for the good
   C) An increase in the price for the good
   D) A shortage of the good
   E) A surplus of the good

The correct answer is B:) An increase in the supply of the good. Technology makes it easier to product a good so there is an increase in the supply of the good.

16) Taxes cause the supply curve to shift

   A) Left
   B) Right
   C) Up
   D) Down
   E) Not at all

The correct answer is A:) Left. This is because they increase the price.

17) Which of the following is NOT one of the six determinants of demand?

   A) Income
   B) Population
   C) Consumer profile
   D) Consumer expectations
   E) Price of complementary good

The correct answer is C:) Consumer profile. The six determinants of demand are taste or preference, income, substitution effect, price of complementary goods, population and consumer expectations.

18) Craig's Diamond Jewelry has been doing well, but they take a financial hit and are able to produce less jewelry. Even so, they charge the same amount for what they do produce. This is a

   A) Left shift
   B) Right shift
   C) Upward shift
   D) Complete curve change
   E) Movement along the curve

The correct answer is E:) Movement along the curve. They are charging the same proportional amount, therefore it is a movement along the curve.

19) Which of the following does NOT shift the supply curve to the right or left?

   A) Technology
   B) Number of suppliers
   C) Government
   D) Demand
   E) Input prices

The correct answer is D:) Demand. Input prices, producer's expectations, technology, the change in the price of other goods, the number of suppliers, and the government can shift the supply curve to the right of left.

20) Over time ATC will

   A) Decrease quickly then increase slowly
   B) Increase slowly then decrease quickly
   C) Increase quickly then decrease slowly
   D) Decrease slowly then increase quickly
   E) Level out and decrease slowly

The correct answer is A:) Decrease quickly then increase slowly. The ATC will first decrease dramatically, as the average fixed and variable costs decrease. However, as time goes on the AFC begins to level out and the AVC may increase. This causes the ATC to level out and then slowly increase as well.

21) What can a government use to create a shortage of a certain good or service?

   A) Importing
   B) Exporting
   C) Taxes
   D) Price ceiling
   E) None of the above

The correct answer is D:) Price ceiling. A price ceiling sets a maximum price for a good or service. When placed under market equilibrium a shortage is created. It is used to encourage people to use a certain good or service.

22) In a pure competition market the companies are called

   A) Price takers
   B) Firms
   C) Establishments
   D) Entities
   E) None of the above

The correct answer is A:) Price takers. Because the companies have little power to change prices they are called price takers.

23) Demand curve slopes

   A) Upward
   B) Downward
   C) Parabolic
   D) Horizontally
   E) Vertically

The correct answer is B:) Downward. The demand curve slope is in a downward direction. The y-axis represents price while the x-axis represents quantity demanded. The downward slope results from more quantity demanded at lower prices.

24) A pet store doubles the price of dogs. If dogs have a price elasticity of supply equal to -.25 how should they change their supply?

   A) Double it
   B) Increase it by 33%
   C) Leave it unchanged
   D) Decrease it by 33%
   E) Cut it in half

The correct answer is E:) Cut it in half. Following the price elasticity of supply formula: -.25(% change in supply)/200% which means % change in supply = (-.25)(200%)=-50%.

25) If the elasticity of demand is greater than 1, then a 5% reduction in price will result in

   A) No change of the quantity demanded
   B) An increase of 2 1/2% in the quantity demanded
   C) An increase of 5% in the quantity demanded
   D) An increase of more than 5% in the quantity demanded
   E) A decrease of more than 5% in the quantity demanded

The correct answer is D:) An increase of more than 5% in the quantity demanded.

26) Two items have a negative cross price elasticity of demand. They are

   A) Abnormal
   B) Complements
   C) Substitutes
   D) Normal goods
   E) None of the above

The correct answer is B:) Complements.

27) The industry demand curve has

   A) Less slope than government demand curves
   B) Less slope than individual demand curves
   C) Equal slope as individual demand curves
   D) More slope than individual demand curves
   E) More slope than government demand curves

The correct answer is B:) Less slope than individual demand curves.

28) Ten years ago an English teacher contacted a workbook provider and asked them to send her all of the workbooks they had. They sent her 1500, each of which cost her 10 dollars. Today she calls the same provider and once against has them send her all of the workbooks they have. This time they send her 750 workbooks and each is 20 dollars. What most likely explains the increased price?

   A) The increased demand
   B) The increased supply
   C) The decreased demand
   D) The decreased supply
   E) None of the above

The correct answer is D:) The decreased supply. Because the supply was lower, and the demand remained the same, they were able to charge more per book.

29) What does elasticity measure?

   A) Responsiveness of price
   B) Flexibility of supply
   C) Stretchability in the market
   D) Fluctuations in the market
   E) The changes in demand

The correct answer is A:) Responsiveness of price. Elasticity shows how a change in supply or demand effects the price of different services or goods.

30) In which of the following cases is an absolute advantage demonstrated?

I.   A sister is better than her brother at cooking, but he is better at fixing cars.
II. One company both manufactures and repairs products better and faster than any other company.
III. A race horse has never lost a race and holds the speed record for his category.

   A) I only
   B) II and III only
   C) I and II only
   D) II only
   E) I, II and III

The correct answer is E:) I, II and III. All of the answers demonstrate an instance in which one person is better than another at something. Although in answer I it is not one of the two who is better at both things, it is still absolute advantage because each is clearly better at something specific.

31) Price elasticity is unaffected by which of the following?

   A) Market equilibrium price
   B) Time
   C) Number of close substitutes
   D) Personal value of the good
   E) Percent of income spent on the good

The correct answer is A:) Market equilibrium price. Price elasticity of demand is determined by changes in time, the number of close substitutes, the personal value of the good and the percent of income spent on the good.

32) Which of the following is NOT a characteristic of public goods?

   A) Easy availability
   B) Essentially unlimited
   C) Free
   D) Equally available
   E) All of the above are characteristics of public goods

The correct answer is E:) All of the above are characteristics of public goods.

33) If the result to the cross-elasticity equation is a negative number, the goods are

   A) Nonexistent
   B) Substitute
   C) Complementary
   D) Inferior
   E) Independent

The correct answer is C:) Complementary. Complementary goods result in a negative number in the cross elasticity equation.

34) An increased demand for pizza prompts a pizza company to buy a wheat field so they can produce more crust. This would happen in a(n)

   A) Labor market
   B) Monopolistic competition market
   C) Prisoner's Dilemma
   D) Subsidized market
   E) Factor market

The correct answer is E:) Factor market. In factor markets, the interest is placed in resources.

35) An improvement in production technology for a certain good leads to

    A) An increase in the demand for a good
    B) An increase in supply of the good
    C) An increase in the price of a good
    D) A shortage of the good
    E) A surplus of the good

The correct answer is B:) An increase in supply of the good.

36) Which of the following is NOT a characteristic of a monopolistic competition market?

    A) Many buyers and sellers in the market
    B) All companies produce similar but different products
    C) All companies coordinate prices for mutual benefits
    D) Consumers have extensive knowledge about product
    E) Relatively no entrance barriers or restrictions

The correct answer is C:) All companies coordinate prices for mutual benefits. A monopolistic competition market is characterized by companies all attempting to maximize their own profit, with little regard for prices of other companies.

37) Between 1980 and 1990, which of the following countries grew the most rapidly?

    A) Japan
    B) China
    C) Russia
    D) United States
    E) Brazil

The correct answer is A:) Japan.

38) Which type of market is the standard to which markets are compared?

    A) Monopolistic competition
    B) Pure competition
    C) Monopolies
    D) Oligopolies
    E) Industrial

The correct answer is B:) Pure competition.

39) Unemployment is prevalent during

   A) Boom
   B) Depression
   C) War
   D) Growth
   E) Post-war

The correct answer is B:) Depression.

40) Which of the following is an inferior good?

   A) Cars
   B) Houses
   C) Jewelry
   D) Clothes
   E) None of the above

The correct answer is E:) None of the above. In all of the examples, it is likely that as a person's income increases, they will have a higher demand for the item.

41) A moderate rate of inflation, such as 35% per annum

   A) Hurts people living on fixed incomes
   B) Helps people living on fixed incomes
   C) Results in no changes
   D) Improves credit scores
   E) None of the above

The correct answer is A:) Hurts people living on fixed incomes. When inflation rises, most of the people living on fixed incomes do not receive a cost of living increase or adjustment and are then able to buy less with the same amount of money.

42) There are four competing companies in the world which sell a specialized brand of mattresses. These four companies one day agree to work together and set the price for the mattresses at a similar and high price. This is an example of a(n)

   A) ATC
   B) Substitute
   C) Oligopoly
   D) Cartel
   E) Pure competition market

The correct answer is D:) Cartel. The four companies were an oligopoly, but when they began working together they became a cartel.

43) Gresham's law says that

   A) All money is bad
   B) Money is the root of all evil
   C) Bad money drives out the good
   D) Money will not make you happy
   E) None of the above

The correct answer is C:) Bad money drives out the good.

44) In order to be effective, a price floor must be

   A) Higher than market equilibrium
   B) Lower than market equilibrium
   C) At market equilibrium
   D) Half market equilibrium
   E) None of the above

The correct answer is A:) Higher than market equilibrium. Otherwise the price floor would have no effect.

45) What is the most important characteristic of perfect competition?

   A) Alike firms
   B) Advertising restrictions
   C) Collusion agreements
   D) Product aggregation reports
   E) Price is set by the industry's supply and demand

The correct answer is E:) Price is set by the industry's supply and demand.

46) A pizza company is going to introduce a new type of pizza. They are considering a meat lovers, vegetarian, six cheese, and pepperoni with a cheese filled crust. After much deliberation, they decide to take a vote. The pepperoni with a cheese filled crust just barely beats six cheese. Six cheese is followed by vegetarian. What is the opportunity cost?

   A) Pepperoni with cheese filled crust
   B) Vegetarian
   C) Meat lover's
   D) Six cheese
   E) A combination of vegetarian, meat lover's and six cheese

The correct answer is D:) Six cheese. In determining opportunity cost, it is the second choice which matters.

47) Incomes are determined in the markets primarily for

   A) Factors of production
   B) Wages and salaries
   C) Marginal private costs
   D) Black market
   E) World price

The correct answer is A:) Factors of production.

48) Subsidies cause the demand curve to shift

   A) Down
   B) Up
   C) Right
   D) Left
   E) Not at all

The correct answer is C:) Right. This means that the price decreases and the demand increases.

49) During the past decade, the Federal Government has

   A) Increased inflation
   B) Closed markets
   C) Run a deficit every year
   D) Imposed price ceilings
   E) None of the above

The correct answer is C:) Run a deficit every year.

50) In the long run, the average variable cost will

   A) Vary unpredictably
   B) Increase and then decrease
   C) Decrease and then increase
   D) Decrease proportional to production
   E) Level off and then rapidly increase

The correct answer is C:) Decrease and then increase.

51) The law of diminishing marginal utility tells us that marginal utility

   A) May rise at first but will eventually fall
   B) May fall at first but will eventually rise
   C) Stays constant over time
   D) Drops on a seasonal basis
   E) None of the above

The correct answer is A:) May rise at first but will eventually fall.

52) Which of the following is NOT a characteristic of perfect competition markets?

   A) No entrance barriers or restrictions
   B) Several large companies in competition
   C) Identical products sold by all companies
   D) Perfect knowledge about the product
   E) No exit barriers or restrictions

The correct answer is B:) Several large companies in competition. A perfect competition market has many small companies, not large companies.

53) The characteristic of fixed costs are

   A) They are predetermined by industry
   B) Marginal
   C) They are always fixed
   D) They are fixed only in the short run
   E) None of the above

The correct answer is D:) They are fixed only in the short run.

54) BMWs have a cross price elasticity of 2. They are

   A) Inelastic
   B) Irregular
   C) Normal
   D) Inferior
   E) Expensive

The correct answer is C:) Normal. Normal goods have a positive cross price elasticity greater than one.

55) An industry under perfect competition has

   A) So many buyers and sellers that none can influence price
   B) So few buyers and sellers that none can influence price
   C) So many buyers that none can influence price
   D) So many sellers that none can influence price
   E) So few buyers that none can influence price

The correct answer is A:) So many buyers and sellers that none can influence price.

56) A grocery store knows that their large supply of meat is about to go bad, so they lower the price dramatically. After doing so it all sells out in one day. How did the demand change?

   A) It went from high to low
   B) It stayed fairly constant
   C) It went from low to high
   D) It varied indescribably
   E) Cannot be determined

The correct answer is C:) It went from low to high. This happened as a result of the price changing from higher to lower.

57) To be effective, a perfectly competitive market needs

   A) Some benefits of the good to go to its consumers
   B) All benefits of the good to go to its consumers
   C) Market diversification
   D) Benefits in society
   E) None of the above

The correct answer is B:) All benefits of the good to go to its consumers.

58) Which type of market is characterized by the dominance of a few large companies?

   A) Monopolistic competition
   B) Pure competition
   C) Monopoly
   D) Oligopoly
   E) Industrial

The correct answer is D:) Oligopoly.

59) A monopoly has

   A) Problems impacting consumption
   B) Increases in labor activity
   C) Allocative and technical inefficiency
   D) Tolerable competition levels
   E) None of the above

The correct answer is C:) Allocative and technical inefficiency.

60) Which of the following is NOT a characteristic of private goods?

   A) Exclusion
   B) Rivalry
   C) Limit
   D) Free
   E) All of the above

The correct answer is D:) Free. Private goods are sold for a specified price to a consumer.

61) Product differentiation is the main characteristic of

   A) Monopolistic competition
   B) Oligopoly
   C) Monarchy
   D) Monopoly
   E) Franchise

The correct answer is A:) Monopolistic competition.

62) A person interviews with a company, knowing that they have 100 other applicants. This type of market is most correctly described as a(n)

   A) Oligopoly
   B) Factor market
   C) Industrial market
   D) Labor Market
   E) Perfect competition market

The correct answer is D:) Labor market. In a labor market, employees compete for jobs and employers compete for employees.

63) If a government prevents a natural monopoly formation it may result in

   A) Collusion
   B) Curbing benefits of economies of scale
   C) Monetary flow
   D) Inflation
   E) Price ceilings

The correct answer is B:) Curbing benefits of economies of scale.

64) A company has a price elasticity of supply which is equal to -2 for their product. A communication error causes an accidental 20% production increase. How must the company change their price to match the new supply?

   A) Increase by 20%
   B) Increase by 10%
   C) Leave it unchanged
   D) Decrease by 10%
   E) Decrease by 20%

The correct answer is D:) Decrease by 10%. Using the formula elasticity of supply = (% change in supply)/(% change inSSS price) we determine -2=(20%)/(% change in price) and % change in price=-10%.

65) The practice of keeping works who are not needed is referred to as

   A) Reverse layoffs
   B) Crowding
   C) Arbitrage
   D) Feather bedding
   E) Discounting

The correct answer is D:) Feather bedding.

66) Which of the following sets of products most likely has a positive cross price elasticity of demand?

   A) Pizza and soda
   B) Paper and pencils
   C) MP3 players and music
   D) Chips and dip
   E) Energy drinks and soda

The correct answer is E:) Energy drinks and soda. Of the answer choices the products in E are the most likely substitutes, which indicates that they have a positive cross price elasticity of demand.

67) In a Lorenze curve, if the bow is larger it denotes

　　A) Inflation
　　B) Quantity demanded
　　C) Quantity supplied
　　D) Equality of income
　　E) Inequality of income

The correct answer is E:) Inequality of income.

68) To be effective a price ceiling must be

　　A) Higher than market equilibrium
　　B) Lower than market equilibrium
　　C) At market equilibrium
　　D) Double market equilibrium
　　E) None of the above

The correct answer is B:) Lower than market equilibrium. Otherwise it would have no effect.

69) A public good

　　A) Benefits all
　　B) Benefits some
　　C) Benefits none
　　D) Benefits government
　　E) None of the above

The correct answer is A:) Benefits all.

70) What is it called when two prisoners are separated for questioning and offered deals with reduced sentences?

　　A) Oligopolic strategy
　　B) Prisoner's Dilemma
　　C) Nash Equilibrium
　　D) Sadistic externality
　　E) None of the above

The correct answer is B:) Prisoner's Dilemma. This is a popular type of game theory.

71) When a company produces a similar product as a competitor it is called

   A) Monopolistic competition
   B) Oligopoly
   C) Monopoly
   D) Monarchy
   E) None of the above

The correct answer is A:) Monopolistic competition.

72) A shoe store is in competition with another shoe store in the area and it goes out of business. As a result, they are able to make a left shift in their supply curve. This means they

   A) Have a one week shoe sale.
   B) Decrease the price of all their shoes.
   C) Raise the price of all their shoes.
   D) Both A and C
   E) None of the above

The correct answer is C:) Raise the price of all their shoes.

73) The center or middle number is a distribution

   A) Mean
   B) Average
   C) Mode
   D) Median
   E) None of the above

The correct answer is D:) Median.

74) If the price of an iPod decreases from 200 dollars to 150 dollars, and the cross price elasticity of demand between iPods and music is -2, then how will the demand for music change?

   A) Increased by 25%
   B) Decreased by 25%
   C) Increased by 50%
   D) Decreased by 50%
   E) Cannot be determined without more information

The correct answer is C:) Increased by 50%. The price of an iPod changed by -25%. Using the formula this means that (% change in demand for music)/-25%=-2, so the demand changed by (-25%)(-2)=50%. A 50% increase.

75) When there is only one seller of a product in the market it is called

   A) Monopolistic competition
   B) Oligopoly
   C) Monopoly
   D) Monarchy
   E) None of the above

The correct answer is C:) Monopoly.

76) Scarcity occurs when

   A) Supply is greater than demand
   B) Demand is greater than supply
   C) A product is a normal good
   D) A product is an inferior good
   E) None of the above

The correct answer is B:) Demand is greater than supply.

77) The interest rate that the Federal Reserve charges to banks is called

   A) Discount rate
   B) Debt rate
   C) Deflation rate
   D) Demand rate
   E) None of the above

The correct answer is A:) Discount rate.

78) Which of the following describes a positive externality?

   A) When a financial benefit comes to a person or group from another person outside the company.
   B) When a financial cost comes to a person or group from another person outside the company.
   C) When a person's or group's activities cause benefits for a person outside the company.
   D) When a person's or group's activities bring costs to people outside the company.
   E) None of the above

The correct answer is C:) When a person's or group's activities cause benefits for a person outside the company.

79) Which of the following benefit from inflation?

   A) Governments
   B) Creditors
   C) Debtors
   D) Banks
   E) None of the above

The correct answer is C:) Debtors.

80) Subsidies cause the supply curve to shift

   A) Up
   B) Down
   C) Left
   D) Right
   E) Not at all

The correct answer is D:) Right. This is because they decrease the cost so the producer will increase it to compensate and make more money.

81) A market where there are few companies that fiercely compete for market share is called

   A) Monopolistic competition
   B) Oligopoly
   C) Monopoly
   D) Monarchy
   E) None of the above

The correct answer is B:) Oligopoly.

82) In the long run the average fixed cost will

   A) Vary unpredictably
   B) Increase and then decrease
   C) Decrease and then increase
   D) Decrease proportional to production
   E) Level off and then rapidly decrease

The correct answer is D:) Decrease proportional to production. The formula for average fixed cost is AFC= fixed cost/amount produced.

83) A formal, sometimes written agreement between companies or individuals to cap output and prices to control the market

   A) Cartel
   B) Collusion
   C) Group buying agreement
   D) Club
   E) Co-op

The correct answer is A:) Cartel. While collusion is very similar to a cartel, the important word is formal. Collusion is an informal agreement. OPEC is an example of a cartel. Both collusion and cartels are illegal in the United States.

84) If two products have a cross price elasticity of demand of .1, they are considered

   A) Elastic
   B) Inelastic
   C) Regular
   D) Unrelated
   E) Complements

The correct answer is B:) Inelastic. Two products are considered inelastic if they have a cross price elasticity which is less than one.

85) A company's profit is _____ when marginal revenue equals marginal cost.

   A) Oligopoly
   B) Perfectly competitive
   C) Imperfectly competitive
   D) Monarchy
   E) None of the above

The correct answer is B:) Perfectly competitive.

86) A computer company produces a new type of software that becomes extremely popular, and they sell 50,000 copies. A second company produces a similar product and, expecting to sell a similar amount, makes 50,000 copies as well. However, they sell less than half what the first company did. Which of the fol- lowing best explains why the second company did worse?

   A) Supply decreased
   B) Demand increased
   C) Supply remained constant
   D) Demand decreased
   E) Cannot be determined

The correct answer is D:) Demand decreased. Because so many people already had the product, less people wanted to buy it after the second company released it, therefore the demand decreased.

87) Which of the following is a elasticity range on the demand curve?

   A) Unitary elastic
   B) Sloping downward
   C) Sloping upward
   D) Demand curve spiral
   E) none of the above

The correct answer is A:) Unitary elastic.

88) Taxes cause the demand curve to shift

   A) Right
   B) Left
   C) Down
   D) Up
   E) Not at all

The correct answer is B:) Left. This is because taxes increase the price and decrease the demand.

89) Bryce eats two pieces of pizza, the same as everyone at the table. There is one piece left over, which he is allowed to eat as well. Bryce has just experienced

   A) Utility
   B) Hunger
   C) Marginal utility
   D) Usefulness
   E) None of the above

The correct answer is C:) Marginal utility.

90) MP3 players and stereos both have cross price elasticity's of -2.4. They are

   A) Scarce
   B) Elastic
   C) Normal
   D) Inferior
   E) Expensive

The correct answer is D:) Inferior. Inferior goods have a negative cross price elasticity.

91) Tim is willing to pay $18 for a new DVD. The current sales price is $20. The difference between what Tim is willing and able to pay for the product and the cost of the product is called

    A) Utility
    B) Marginal utility
    C) Explicit costs
    D) Consumer surplus
    E) Implicit costs

The correct answer is D:) Consumer surplus.

92) Minimum wage is an example of

    A) Price floor
    B) Price ceiling
    C) Supply
    D) Demand
    E) None of the above

The correct answer is A:) Price floor. Minimum wage is a government mandated minimum payment.

93) COLA is a

    A) Diet drink
    B) Increase in wages
    C) Government program
    D) Marketing concept
    E) Bond program

The correct answer is B:) Increase in wages. COLA stands for cost-of-living-adjustment.

94) Which of the following describes a negative externality?

   A) When a financial benefit comes to a person or group from another person outside the company.
   B) When a financial cost comes to a person or group from another person outside the company.
   C) When a person's or group's activities cause benefits for a person outside the company.
   D) When a person's or group's activities bring costs to people outside the company.
   E) None of the above

The correct answer is D:) When a person's or group's activities bring costs to people outside the company.

95) A decrease in price levels is called

   A) Deficit
   B) Utility
   C) Deflation
   D) Demand
   E) Implicit costs

The correct answer is C:) Deflation.

96) Which of the following are most likely NOT complements?

   A) Pizza and soda
   B) Paper and pencils
   C) MP3 players and music
   D) Energy drinks and soda
   E) Chips and dip

The correct answer is D:) Energy drinks and soda. The two are most likely substitutes. Since both are drinks it is not likely that they would be bought together.

97) When quantity supply exceeds quantity demand

   A) Excess demand
   B) Excess supply
   C) Revenue
   D) Marginal costs
   E) None of the above

The correct answer is A:) Excess demand.

98) Game theory is an important aspect of which type of market?

   A) Monopolistic competition
   B) Pure competition
   C) Monopoly
   D) Oligopoly
   E) Industrial

The correct answer is D:) Oligopoly. Game theory describes a person's reactions in different situations. Oligopolies are the only market in which competitors closely monitor each other's decisions, and in which strategy is an important factor.

99) _____ is total cost divided by quantity.

   A) Marginal cost
   B) Average total cost
   C) Fixed cost
   D) Variable cost
   E) None of the above

The correct answer is B:) Average total cost.

100) What is long run economic profit for a pure competition market?

   A) Zero
   B) A unique amount for each type of market and each specific market
   C) An amount proportional to the size of the market
   D) An amount proportional to the number of different products
   E) Infinity

The correct answer is A:) Zero.

Test-Taking Strategies

Here are some test-taking strategies that are specific to this test and to other CLEP tests in general:
- Keep your eyes on the time. Pay attention to how much time you have left.
- Read the entire question and read all the answers. Many questions are not as hard to answer as they may seem. Sometimes, a difficult sounding question really only is asking you how to read an accompanying chart. Chart and graph questions are on most CLEP tests and should be an easy free point.
- If you don't know the answer immediately, the new computer-based testing lets you mark questions and come back to them later if you have time.
- Read the wording carefully. Some words can give you hints to the right answer. There are no exceptions to an answer when there are words in the question such as always, all or none. If one of the answer choices includes most or some of the right answers, but not all, then that is not the correct answer. Here is an example:

   The primary colors include all of the following:

   A) Red, Yellow, Blue, Green
   B) Red, Green, Yellow
   C) Red, Orange, Yellow
   D) Red, Yellow, Blue
   E) None of the above

   Although item A includes all the right answers, it also includes an incorrect answer, making it incorrect. If you didn't read it carefully, were in a hurry, or didn't know the material well, you might fall for this.
- Make a guess on a question that you do not know the answer to. There is no penalty for an incorrect answer. Eliminate the answer choices that you know are incorrect. For example, this will let your guess be a 1 in 3 chance instead.

What Your Score Means

Based on your score, you may or may not qualify for credit for your specific institution. At my campus, University of Phoenix, a score of 50 is passing for full credit. At Utah Valley University, the score for credit is unpublished, the school will accept the credit on a case-by-case basis. Nearby, Brigham Young University (BYU) does not accept

CLEP credit. To find out what score you need for credit, you can view it online at www.CLEP.com but you should also verify any information with your school.

You can score between 20 and 80 on any CLEP test. Some exams include percentile ranks. Each correct answer is worth one point. You lose no points for unanswered or incorrect questions.

 Test Preparation

How much you need to study depends on your knowledge of a subject area. If you are interested in literature, took it in school, or enjoy reading then your studying and preparation for the literature or humanities test will not need to be as intensive as for someone who is new to literature.

This book is much different than the regular CLEP study guides. This book actually teaches you the information that you need to know to pass the test. If you are particularly interested in an area, or feel like you want more information, do a quick search online. There is a lot you'll need to memorize. Almost everything in this book will be on the test. It is important to understand all major theories and concepts listed in the table of contents. It is also very important to know any bolded words.

Don't worry if you do not understand or know a lot about the area. If you study hard, you can complete and pass the test.

To prepare for the test, make a series of goals. Allot a certain amount of time to review the information you have already studied and to learn additional material. Take notes as you study-it will help you learn the material.

 Legal Note

All information is copyright of Sheryl Spencer. This manual is not supported by or affiliated with the College Board, creators of the CLEP test. CLEP is a registered trademark of the College Entrance Examination Board, which does not endorse this book.

FLASHCARDS

This section contains flashcards for you to use to further your understanding of the material and test yourself on important concepts, names or dates. Read the term or question then flip the page over to check the answer on the back. Keep in mind that this information may not be covered in the text of the study guide. Take your time to study the flashcards, you will need to know and understand these concepts to pass the test.

The three distinct systems as per principles of economics	Adam Smith's "Wealth of Nations" taught
Principle of relative advantage	Total Utility
Marginal Utility	Law of diminishing marginal utility
Supply and Demand	Excess Demand

Countries should export goods they can make cheaply and import goods that would be expensive to create	Capitalism, socialism and mixed economy
The gross psychological satisfaction a customer receives from consuming a number of goods	A country should take into account which exports would create the most profit
After consuming a certain amount of goods, a customer experiences diminished satisfaction from each good	The psychological satisfaction a customer felt while consuming the most recent unit of a product
When a market wants more of a product that producers are willing to provide	A product's value is higher when demand for the product is high and supply is low

Excess Supply	**Consumer's Surplus**
Elasticity of Demand	**Real Cost**
Explicit Cost	**Money Cost**
Equation used to find the Marginal Revenue	**Perfect Competition**

The difference between the maximum a consumer would pay for a product and the actual price paid in the market	When there is more of a product than the market wants to consume
The amount of mental and physical effort put in and the sacrifices made to produce the commodity	Percentage change in the quantity demanded by the percentage change in the price
The total sum of all factors of production in producing the product	Cash payments made for goods or services
A market with a large number of buyers and sellers of homogenous set of goods	MR= Change in total revenue (TR) / Change in units sold (U)

Monopolistic Competition	**Monopoly**
Derived Demand	**External Economy**
An improvement in production technology leads to:	**Unemployment lurks during**
The author of the theory of comparative advantage is	**Gresham's Law**

Large number of buyers but only one seller	Large numbers of buyers and sellers of a differentiated product
A favorable effect on one or more people that emanates from a different person or firm	When the demand for an input item depends mainly on the demand for the end product it is used to create
Depression	An increase in the supply of the good
Bad money drives out good	David Ricardo

The characteristics of fixed-costs tell us that	Feather bedding is
In a Lorenz curve, if the bow is larger it denotes that	A perfectly competitive market needs
An industry under perfect competition has	Demand curve slopes which way?
Who does a moderate rate of inflation harm?	Net Exports

The practice of keeping workers who are not needed	They are only fixed in the short run
All benefits of a good to go to consumers	A greater degree of inequality of income exists
Downward	So many buyers and sellers that none can influence the price
Exports minus imports	People living on fixed incomes

NOTES

NOTES

NOTES

NOTES

NOTES

NOTES

NOTES

NOTES

NOTES

NOTES

NOTES

NOTES

NOTES

NOTES

NOTES

NOTES

NOTES

NOTES

NOTES

NOTES

NOTES

NOTES

NOTES

NOTES

NOTES

NOTES

NOTES

NOTES

NOTES

NOTES

NOTES

NOTES

NOTES

NOTES

NOTES

NOTES

NOTES

NOTES

NOTES

NOTES

NOTES

NOTES

NOTES

NOTES

NOTES

NOTES